THE HIDDEN ISLAND

THE HIDDEN ISLAND

Essays

ABRAHAM JIMÉNEZ ENOA

Translated by Lily Meyer

Introduction by
Jon Lee Anderson

PUBLISHING
New York, NY

Orginally published by Libros Del KO in Spanish in 2023 as *La Isla Ocula*.

Ig Publishing
Box 2547
New York, NY 10163
www.igpub.com

ISBN: 978-1-63246-209-1

Printed in the United States of America
Manufactuer: Lightning Source

CONTENTS

INTRODUCTION BY JON LEE ANDERSON

For half a century, nearly everything the world learned about Cuba came from the words and deeds of its *jefe máximo*, Fidel Castro, the leader of the "Revolution." He had concentrated all political power in his hands and was the country's only sanctioned authority. In Cuba, if you wanted to know about globalization, the environment, Cuban history, United States history, Che Guevara, Camilo Cienfuegos, nuclear energy, scuba diving, agriculture, dengue fever, José Martí's poetry, or baseball, you had to look no further than Fidel. He knew about everything, including the production of *foie gras*—an obsession of his, for a while—in addition to cattle-breeding, the cultivation of moringa and its putative health benefits. He was a font of wisdom in person and on television, where he'd talk for hours. He held forth at international forums and in lengthy interviews; he delivered the longest speech ever recorded at the United Nations General Assembly—with a duration of two hundred and sixty minutes. And if you missed something he had said, you could always pick up one of the hagiographies his acolytes had published, books like *Fidel and Religion*, *Fidel and Angola*, or *Fidel and Che*, or *One Hundred Hours With Fidel*.

In the early 1990s, the Cuban economy fell into disarray after the implosion of the Soviet Union, which had propped it up for thirty years. Prostitution, which had supposedly been overcome thanks to the Revolution, once again became a visible part of life on the island. Fidel, naturally, had the last word on the matter. He said that he didn't recognize the existence of a sex trade in Cuba, but if one were to exist, he had no doubt that Cuban prostitutes would be "the cleanest and most educated in the world." When I first heard this story, I assumed it was apocryphal. But one day, when I raised the subject with a Cuban government minister, he trotted the line out right away. "On that topic," he told me, "Fidel says—" and he repeated the famous quote.

* * *

Five decades dragged by in that fashion. Anything Fidel hadn't made a pronouncement about was officially ignored. Inconvenient or delicate issues like criminality, HIV/AIDS, suicide, unemployment, drugs, and homosexuality either went unmentioned or were explained away as vestigial evils of "capitalism," which the Revolution would be able to heal if it weren't for the "North American blockade," which was the name officially applied to the trade embargo that the U.S. government had imposed on Cuba after diplomatic relations between the two countries had broken down in 1961.

In his speeches, Fidel used the blockade to explain anything that was otherwise inexplicable in a country blessed by the existence of its good, all-seeing and benevolent Revolution. If there wasn't enough food or fuel to go around, it was because of the blockade imposed by "el imperio," or "The Empire," the government's official moniker for the United States. If Cubans wanted to leave Cuba, it was because of the blockade. If other Cubans protested against the government's curtailment of their civil rights—such as the right to free speech, assembly, and the right to leave the country—they were accused of being agents of the same "Empire" that had imposed the blockade, which meant that they were traitors.

For decades, the imposition of an all-or-nothing worldview helped the Revolution maintain control, but paradoxically, it also created a national perception of Cuba in which its destiny was bound irrevocably to the United States, like the earth orbiting the sun. The U.S. was the behemoth that ultimately determined Cuba's fortunes. And if it was true, as nationalistic Cubans like to say, that all their problems "come from the north," then it followed that the solutions to those problems did, too. According to this logic, the job of improving Cubans' lives wasn't the Revolution's, but the U.S. government's. At a certain point, for instance, Fidel argued that the nefarious Empire had an obligation not only to allow, but to periodically increase, the number of Cubans allowed to emigrate to the United States each year. While Fidel used the aggrieved rhetoric of victimhood, the fact of the matter was that Cuba desperately needed such an escape hatch for its people; if Cubans weren't permitted to leave by plane, they'd take to the sea on rafts.

* * *

Largely left out of the Cuban story during Fidel's decades in power were the personal narratives of ordinary Cubans. In Fidel's telling, there were two kinds of Cubans, both lumped into group categories: the stoic heroes who had stayed, and the *gusanos*, the worms, traitors, and the gangsters, who had fled the island. Of course, time has chipped away at those rigid Cold War classifications, and in the recent post-Fidel years, as Cubans have grown increasingly eager to reclassify and describe themselves as individuals, the rest of the world has grown increasingly eager to listen to them, to hear their stories, and to know who they really are.

Over the years, some Cuban writers and journalists have tried to provide realistic rather than didactic visions of Cuba in their novels and essays, but the consequence for doing that has meant that most had to leave the country or else stay home and be silent. Some, at different times, have done both. Among the names in this long, sad story are Guillermo Cabrera Infante, Heberto Padilla, Virgilio Piñera, Reinaldo Arenas, Carlos Franqui, Norberto Fuentes, and Wendy Guerra. There are many more. A very small group number have managed to cling to their careers inside Cuba, riding first the highs and lows of Fidel's long tenure, then the decade of relative openness during his younger brother Raúl's presidency, followed by the uncertain current post-Castroist era of President Miguel Díaz-Canel. Amongst them, literary veterans Pedro Juan Gutiérrez and Leonardo Padura learned how to survive by avoiding any direct criticism of the Revolution in their writings and watching their mouths when they're at home.

* * *

Cuba also has a new literary generation, one in which Abraham Jiménez Enoa, the author of this collection of essays, is an important figure. He and his fellows are in their mid-thirties, born at the end of the Cold War. They were raised not during the Cuban Revolution's golden age, the era of *Socialism or Death* and *Venceremos*, but in the time of its deterioration and decrepitude. The son of a military family, Abraham studied journalism at the University of Havana and graduated in the mid-2010s during the brief cultural opening that occurred after Raúl Castro and Barack Obama restored relations between Cuba and the U.S. after a half-century's freeze.

Encouraged by the permissive new atmosphere and further

empowered by the Cuban government's decision to make internet access widely available, Abraham and a few friends launched their own digital online media outlet, which they called *El Estornudo*, or The Sneeze. They introduced it as an "independent magazine of narrative journalism," and it swiftly gained a readership—albeit one mostly outside of Cuba. *El Estornudo* was something completely new. At a moment when the outside world wanted to learn more about Cuba, it offered serious original reporting, sharp commentary, and intelligent analyses of Cuban society, and it was coming from youthful Cubans who'd never had a public voice before. Best of all, its writers still lived on the island, not in Miami or Madrid.

* * *

Cuba's détente with the U.S. was barely two years old when Donald Trump won the 2016 presidential election, and once installed in the White House, wasted no time undoing the renewed American relationship with Cuba. Simultaneously, diplomats and intelligence agents in the U.S. embassy in Havana began suffering a series of mysterious "acoustic attacks" that damaged the health of those targeted. Hardliners in Cuba's government, meanwhile, stepped back from the opening with the U.S. and put the brakes on the internal glasnost it had fostered.

El Estornudo still publishes today, but none of its founders still live in Cuba. Reimposing strict control over the national discourse, Cuba's censors forced them—one after another—out of the country in retaliation for their lucidity, their dark humor, and their critical analyses. *El Estornudo's* writers had done their obligatory postgraduate national service at Cuba's official media outlets like *Granma*, *Juventud Rebelde*, and *Trabajadores*, but the government could no longer tolerate them once they sought to have independent voices.

Abraham Jiménez Enoa was the last of his *Estornudo* friends to leave Cuba. He had done his own national service at a publication of the Ministry of the Interior, and because of that, on supposed national security grounds, he was prohibited from leaving Cuba for six long years. The restriction launched a new phase in his life. Since he was forbidden to leave his country or to express himself freely within it, Abraham began writing about his cloistered existence in an unabashed monthly column for the *Washington Post*. In an attempt to intimiate him into silence, Cuban state security surveilled his movements and periodically detained, interrogated, and threatened him.

When the "migratory regulation" stricture that had entrapped him in Cuba was finally lifted in 2021, Abraham secured a passport and left the country, like so many Cubans had done before him. He now lives in Barcelona. He is thirty-seven, and a father. Now that he's able to speak freely, he is free to share this remarkable collection of essays. *The Hidden Island* shows us a Cuba naked in all its shame and glory. We see everything here: a memorable profile of a female boxer, the story of a gigolo, and another about an internet troll in the regime's employ. We meet homeless Cubans and pushcart vendors eking out a living by selling fruit and vegetables from dawn to dusk, all of them scraping by in a former socialist paradise. We also see Abraham's heartrending departure from Cuba. He narrates his shock upon arriving in the "outside" world, which not only has everything that Cuba does not have, but has it to a dizzying excess. "Leaving Cuba," he writes, "isn't like leaving any other country. Leaving Cuba means landing in the world. It shows you beyond a doubt that Cuba has been held hostage in the twentieth century by a political system that won't allow it to advance."

Abraham has an admirable social conscience and he writes like an angel. He's also Afro-Cuban, which is to say that he's Black, and when he writes about discrimination in his society, he knows what he's talking about. He is an exceptional interlocutor, and, for readers of this unmissable book, he is an honest and compassionate guide to Cuba, a country as beautiful and beloved as it is sad and unjust.

THE AQUATICS' REVOLUTION

Cries of pain shake the house. A cloth curtain hangs from the wooden ceiling, hiding the room where the cries come from. The curtain sways occasionally, moved by the summer wind and the shrieks that split the dawn. In this unhappy room, it sounds, from the high wailing that wrecks the idyll of this plain in the Viñales Valley's Sierra del Infierno, like some wounded beast has come to die.

Out in the living room, Juanito and Victoria's children and their spouses—all ten of them—sit on wooden rockers and armchairs around the dining table, elbows on knees, faces in hands. Nobody speaks. Between the cries, it's quiet except for the insufferable hum of the giant white-footed mosquitos swarming everywhere and the rhythmic croak of frogs celebrating the drizzle outside. Each cry from the next room echoes on the damp wood of the house, slicing like knives into the family's starved faces, which are frozen like masks until the next moan makes them draw their eyebrows down, harden their cheeks and clench their jaws until their teeth touch.

In the curtained bedroom, eighty-two-year-old Juanito lies on a bare mattress. His wife, Victoria, age eighty, stands beside him, wet-eyed, running her hand silently over his torso. They have been married for fifty-four years. A pair of metal bowls sit on the ground, one full of water, the other half-empty. Each bowl contains a rag and a metal cup with no handle.

Juanito asks Victoria to help him sit up. Slowly, their hands intertwined, she helps him upright. She sets the bowl full of water on his thighs. He dips his hands into the water and closes his eyes, slurring inaudible words that could be a prayer. Victoria shuts her own eyes and weeps. Juanito turns his hands into a vessel, scoops up some water, and douses his head, his back, nearly his whole body. He runs the wet rag over his side where the pain from his intestinal hernia and kidney infection is at its worst, before sinking back down into the mattress.

Juanito immediately starts sweating so hard he looks like a melting chunk of ice. Soon his expressions of pain and anguish return, disfiguring his face. His mouth twists; his eyes turn up and roll; his teeth dig into the thin, dry meat of his lips. Once again, the house rattles with his cries. His whole family is here, but none of them try to get a doctor to calm his suffering. For more than eighty years, nothing has healed Juanito except water.

* * *

Juanito was born in 1935 in the Cayos de San Felipe, an isolated community in Pinar del Río, a province in Cuba's Guaniguanico mountain range that became a UNESCO biosphere reserve in 1999.

Juanito was a sickly child. At the age of two, he weighed only thirteen pounds. His lungs barely worked. Anything his parents could scrape from their small farm, with its handful of work animals, went toward specialists and medications, none of which helped. Eventually, the doctors told his parents to stop wasting their resources. They said that Juanito's lungs hadn't developed correctly in utero, and that he didn't have long to live.

But change was coming to the Cayos de San Felipe because of a local woman named Antoñica Izquierdo. A mother of seven, Antoñica was overtaken with despair at her powerlessness to help her youngest son, who was suffering from the sudden illnesses simply called "fevers" in those days. She and her husband couldn't afford the journey from their rocky, rural home to a doctor who could treat their son. So Antoñica left the boy on his bed of palm leaves, and went to her altar, where she begged God for help. While she was gone, her husband held their child, who was trembling so badly both of them shook.

Hours later, Antoñica returned. "I spoke to the Virgin," she told her husband. "She told me how to save our son." She quickly peeled the boy's clothes off, wrapped him in white rags and carried him through the dark mountain night to a nearby creek. There, she plunged him into the water and bathed him, praying the whole time. On the walk home, the boy's body cooled down. It was January 8, 1936, and as far as Antoñica and her husband were concerned, a miracle had taken place: the fever was gone.

Antoñica later claimed to have been blessed with a second divine apparition, after which she announced, "I am the Virgin Mary's appointed protector of the wretched of the earth, designated to heal and cure them without self-interest, without asking for a cent, without using medicine—only with water."

Before long, the Cayos de San Felipe was transformed from an impenetrable tangle of hills, brambles and greedy red mud into a site of incessant pilgrimages. People beat paths through the thickets and massed outside the home of Antoñica Izquierdo, the water healer.

In 1937, Juanito's parents took him to meet Antoñica. So many people thronged around her palm-roofed house that they had to wait several days to see her. When they finally did, Juanito says, she looked hard at him and told his parents, "Don't give this boy any more medicine. Bathe him in the spring for nine days."

Before visiting Antoñica, Juanito's parents had made a vow: if she healed their son, the family would never see a doctor again. After being bathed, Juanito wasn't just healed, but healthy. His father lived to ninety-two, his mother ninety-three, with water as their only medicine.

* * *

Only weeks before he took to bed in pain, Juanito was working the fields as usual. At eighty-two, he's long been used to the bullying sun, wearing a wide palm-leaf hat and a soldier's olive drab shirt and pants to protect himself. No shoes. Juanito is a gentle, laughing man, hard of hearing and blind in his left eye. A peasant whose body bears the scars of a lifetime of labor. His hair, once light, is now dark brown and his formerly pale skin is lined and coppery. His palms and the soles of his feet are pure steel.

Despite his age and physical limitations, Juanito still chooses to get up at dawn and join his children in the tobacco fields, or in the plots where they grow yucca, taro, beans and corn. He gets home around two in the afternoon, his clothes soaked with sweat, his feet caked with mud. Days before his agony begins, he stands on the threshold of his home after a morning of work and says, "I was on death's door as a boy. According to the doctors, I had no hope, but Antoñica cured me—and look at me now, after eighty years. Our belief is healthy. It's rooted in our faith in water. We understand that, in the end, a person who's going to die will die, no matter how many doctors they have."

* * *

In April 1936, Antoñica was taken from her home in full view of a crowd of people bunched tightly together, waiting to be cured.

It had been raining for days, and the pilgrims, who had nowhere to take shelter, were sleeping outside. According to *The Days of Water*, a 1971 film about Antoñica, the authorities arrested the water healer and accused her of killing a man whose body was found decomposing next to a creek. Pinning his death on her suited both Pinar del Río's politicians and its doctors, who, newspapers reported at the time, were threatened by Antoñica and her practices.

At her trial, Antoñica declared, "I'd rather be called a murderer than let anyone say God isn't a healer or isn't working miracles through me." By then, her fame was so great that a lawyer named Navarro, a major political player in Pinar del Río in the 1930s, based his campaign for Senate—which he won, beating the incumbent, Pedro Blanco, by a wide margin—on getting Antoñica out of prison. Navarro defended Antoñica, and she was ultimately found not guilty.

This victory would cost Antoñica her life.

After she was released from prison, Antoñica returned home and continued healing the needy, including Juanito. But she remained a target of the Cuban establishment—so much so that she instructed her faithful to burn their identity documents, quit any political parties or social groups they belonged to, throw their medicines in the trash and never again set foot or allow their children to set foot in a hospital, school or job center. From then on, she was not only a water healer, but a guide and spiritual protector to her followers.

Antoñica lived on land that belonged to the one-time senator Pedro Blanco. Bitter at his defeat to Navarro, Blanco took revenge by expelling the healer and her adherents from his property. A brutal conflict followed. Many aquatics died fighting the senator's men, while others fled the Cayos de San Felipe.

Antoñica was taken captive once again and sent to Mazorra, a mental institution in Havana, where she spent the rest of her life. According to the psychiatrists there, she was gravely deluded and suffered from visions. She died in 1945, in a room with wet, moldy walls and only one small, iron-barred window to let in sunlight.

Meanwhile, her followers who had escaped Blanco's whip-bearing overseers carried their possessions through Cuba's western mountain ranges, drifting like zombies until they reached an area even harder to penetrate than the Cayos de San Felipe: the Sierra del Infierno. They dynamited one of the region's *mogotes*, or freestanding hills. Once it was destroyed, they cleared a trail leading to a mountain so steep it could only be climbed by foot or horse. On that mountain, the aquatics created a community that was isolated from the world, just as Antoñica had wanted.

Several years passed, and in 1959, Fidel Castro and his bearded rebels took power. News of the Revolution didn't reach the aquatics for a long time, and it didn't matter to them when it did. In their community, politicians and institutions were irrelevant. Their biggest issue was transporting and burying their dead, as everyone had grown tired of carrying coffins down miles of mountain trails.

After Castro declared Cuba a socialist nation, the aquatics' part of the Sierra del Infierno and the U.S. military base at Guantánamo became the only pieces of the island that the Revolution wouldn't touch. Today, seventy-five years after Antoñica Izquierdo's death, aquatic families still cure themselves with water rather than going to doctors or hospitals; still refuse to engage with the Cuban state, carry ID, or join social groups; and still don't send their children to school, though most permit them to learn to read and write. However, the passage of time threatens their faith, as aquatics—especially young ones—who travel to the lowlands and encounter the advances of modernity rarely return to their narrow rural lives.

After migrating from the Cayos de San Felipe to the Sierra del Infierno, the aquatic community grew to twenty-seven families. Today there are only two left, broken into eight households. More aquatics live in the town of Viñales, still maintaining their beliefs after abandoning life in the mountains. Others have gone even further, creating a new community in the rural section of the municipality of San Cristóbal, in the province of Artemisa. At one point, there were 1,000 aquatics in San Cristóbal, the biggest population on record. Now, 70 families, or about 200 people, remain.

* * *

So much water runs though the Sierra del Infierno's underground springs that, instead of shrinking from the sunlight, the mud defies and defeats it. Some paths are so rocky and wet that even the horses have to tread carefully; others are just swamps of red mud where the horses rear and toss their heads as they go.

But off the trails, the Sierra is peaceful. All you hear is the wind and the birds trilling as they flutter from branch to dewy green branch. Below is the Viñales Valley with its imposing stone *mogotes*. Halfway up the slope is a plateau, a resting spot. It's the only straight section of the path, and the only part with hard ground. On either side of the trail are dozens of mango trees, whose aroma curls playfully into your nose.

Black chickens pop from the bushes, pursued by tiny chicks whose feathers are a marbled mix of yellow and black. A working dog runs, tongue flapping, after a small crowd of pigs, herding them through a barn door. Someone has notched triangles into the dog's ears to prevent mange. Milagro and Berto, an aquatic couple, live nearby. Milagro, fifty, is a stout, light-skinned woman with short hair and an elusive manner. Anything that sounds like a question makes her frown. She's tense around anyone who isn't from the mountain. Berto is small and brown-skinned, still athletic at fifty-one. He wears glasses and a wide-brimmed hat, and though he's friendly, he barely talks. Getting a single sentence out of him is a struggle.

Milagro and Berto rarely go down the mountain. Unless they have a sick relative to see or need a new part for their fridge, fan or television, they stay on their property, where their only visitors are family members who come up from the lowlands, the hired hand who knocks on the door before starting his daily chores and the tourists who hike the Sierra to look at the valley from above to catch a glimpse of the aquatics' life. "It helps when tourists come," Milagro says, "but the land supports us. Most of our crops, we eat."

In addition to cultivating yucca, corn and taro, the couple and their lone worker juice three tanks' worth of criollo mangoes every morning, skinning hundreds of fruits with small, sharp knives before cutting them into chunks that cover their fingers with thick, sticky threads of juice. They crush the peeled mangoes between wooden rollers and heat the resulting juice over a low flame for forty minutes so that it doesn't ferment. You can buy it, or their homemade lemonade, for one dollar per bottle.

Milagro and Berto live in a stucco house with one solar panel. It took them twenty-seven years to build the house. They hauled the construction materials up the mountain by oxen while living in a palm-roof shack that still stands next to the house. "You wouldn't guess," Berto says, "but that house is better for storms than the stucco one. It's gotten us through tornadoes."

Five families still lived on the mountain in 2008. But then Hurricanes Gustav and Ike hit Pinar del Río, devastating the Sierra del Infierno. "We all lost our roofs and our crops," Berto shares, "and so three families went down the mountain." Those families still maintained their faith, like the aquatics who descended earlier. Milagros notes that "it was the difficulty of life on the mountain that drove them away, but they brought the water with them. They ran a pipe from the spring to their houses in town." Milagro says that many non-aquatics climb the mountain to drink spring water, "to get cured." She adds that she and Berto have no documents identifying them as Cuban citizens, but if a cop asks them for ID on one of their rare visits to the lowlands, they only have to say they're aquatics to be let go.

* * *

"I have never taken medicine in my life," Milagro declares. "If I get sick or feel pain, I soak rags in water and put them where it hurts."

Berto chimes in, "A person's faith goes a long way. My cousin broke his foot recently, and I splinted it with water. He's already walking."

Aquatics treat everything with water. Birth is no exception, though the Cuban Ministry of Health launched an initiative in the 1980s to monitor pregnant women. Once labor starts, women—even those who would prefer not to—must go to a maternity hospital. Or as Milagro puts it disdainfully, lowering her gaze, "when they hear someone's having a baby, the cops and doctors come and drag her to a hospital in town."

Milagro and Berto have two children. Their daughter, age

twenty-eight, was born in a maternity hospital after provincial authorities, tipped off by the police, forced Milagro down the mountain in front of a shocked, weeping Berto. "I didn't want to go," she remembers. "And my daughter has never been healthy since she was born in that hospital."

Their son, who's twenty-one, was born at home. While pregnant, Milagro hid her belly and dodged the nurses who came up the mountain; once she could no longer pretend she wasn't having a baby, she began hiding in the woods. "I'd wake up and go alone into the trees until it got dark and I could come home," she says. She managed to escape the health workers, had her baby at home, and gave him his first bath in the spring. "I tried to teach them our faith, but it wasn't an obligation," Berto says curtly and resentfully. Neither of their children lives on the mountain or is an aquatic.

"It was their decision to go," Milagro says. "It's why there are so few of us now."

* * *

"Antoñica knew that people would trade their religion for the bright lights of the world. She said it would happen the same way it did before the Flood: the faithful would decrease in number," explains Izquierdo's great-nephew Bernardo, leaning on a windowsill in his uncle's house. Bernardo is forty-nine but looks like an old—but healthy—man. His features—hooked nose, taut lips revealing sharp piranha teeth—are intimidating, as is his gaze. His eyes are large and oval, and both his hair and eyebrows are turning white.

He is part of the Rodríguez family, the other aquatic clan that remains in the Sierra del Infierno. Bernardo, who lives in San Cristóbal, is visiting. He had to limp up the mountain; two months ago, while repairing his toilet, he tripped and fell, slicing the tendons in his left foot. His scar is fresh and badly tended, with dead skin still clinging to it. Volcanoes of pus suppurate from the wound. Bernardo says he's treated it with water, water, and more water—and that it's starting to heal. "God created nature, and that's what we trust," he says. "We don't carry state ID because Antoñica told us the Earth would have only two parties: that of God and that of man."

On the side of the Rodríguez home is a solar panel. It was given to them by the state, and supplies just enough power to light the house at night and power the only two electronic devices the family owns: a radio and a refrigerator..

The Rodríguezes were all born on the mountain, without doctors, and they are all still aquatics. Bernardo's uncle, Antonio, owns a pair of black-and-white photos showing Antoñica sitting among her seven kids. Bernardo came up the mountain to see Antonio, who'd been bedridden with kidney pain for days. "I prayed and put wet rags over my kidneys," Antonio says proudly, "and a couple days later, I went to the bathroom and passed a stone. After that, the pain was gone."

In the field outside his uncle's house, Bernardo points out a decapitated boa more than a yard long. He cut its head off with his machete. "We've had much bigger," he says, "but we don't need to fear them. A person can do anything with faith."

* * *

Atop the Sierra del Infierno is a palm-roofed shack where a pair of aquatic cousins, Juan Carlos and Félix, sell cold water, soda and local beers that the hikers drink while appreciating the stunning view of the valley. Neither cousin lives on the mountain, but Juan Carlos, twenty-seven, says that, "religion is in the heart. Where you live isn't important. It's not like you have to sign some contract."

Juan Carlos hardly looks like an aquatic. He has waist-length blond hair and does not dress like a farmer. (He's a mountain guide.) At a glance, he appears to have all his teeth, which the other aquatics don't. Five years ago, he had a romance with a Portuguese tourist he met while leading an expedition. Eventually, they married, and he plans on leaving Cuba soon.

Neither Juan Carlos nor his cousin Félix, forty-three, went to school. Both are semi-literate. Félix says, not bitterly, "I've never minded. In life, you learn as you go." But he adds, "it does keep young people from continuing our tradition. My daughter's boyfriend isn't an aquatic, and I bet someday she's going to go to the doctor or do something else that isn't in our faith."

Félix's daughter, who is now a teenager, learned to read and write from Marcelino Collara Martínez, a fifty-one-year-old teacher the Ministry of Education dispatched to the mountain seventeen years ago. Twice a week, Marcelino leaves his house at dawn and bikes six rocky miles from the town of Viñales to the base of the Sierra before climbing the mountain on foot to teach three aquatic children—one third grader and two eighth graders—in a roughly built classroom. "I can teach them math and Spanish. No science; nothing to do with the human body or sexuality; and no history, since that would involve teaching evolution," Marcelino says. "I got the course plan approved by the government. It beats not teaching them at all."

Marcelino is tall and lean, like a marathoner who trains at altitude before descending to the city to win races. His limbs are long and sunburned, his mustache thick. "None of the kids are smart or curious," he says. "And none of their families care about anything but reading and writing. After ninth grade, I lose them."

After the Revolution, the government tried to break the aquatics' isolation, even building a school in the Sierra. For decades, the aquatic parents refused to send their children there. In the mid-1980s, a few permitted their kids to learn to read, but the teacher caused trouble. "He fell in love with a married aquatic and took her to live in town with him," Marcelino says. "After that, the community rejected all the teachers who showed up until me."

Marcelino earns 671 pesos, or 30 dollars, a month. When he isn't biking to the mountain or teaching on top of it, he gathers cans, plastics, bottles, cartons and other recyclables to sell by the kilo. Without this extra income, he wouldn't be able to support his family.

* * *

Pedro Luis is a resident of Viñales who has lived alongside aquatics his whole life, though he's not one of them. At seventy, he's an endless fountain of stories about the aquatics he's known in his neighborhood and at the agricultural co-ops and forestry service where he worked. Sitting in his tiny living room, he recalls a man he supervised at one co-op who passed out while plowing: "It was his appendix. We had to rush him out of the field to the hospital, where he had surgery right away. We only remembered he was an aquatic afterward. He could never go home after that. He moved to another town."

In the 1990s, when Pedro Luis worked in the forestry service, his boss was an aquatic. "He can barely walk now. Somebody hit his leg with an ax by mistake, and he tried to cure it with water. It never healed, and now everybody knows him as Antonio with the limp."

One of Pedro Luis's neighbors married an aquatic and went

to live on the mountain: "She got burned all over her body somehow, and instead of taking her to the ER, they left her in bed and put water on her. Within days, maggots ate her while they watched."

But none of Pedro Luis's surreal stories revolt him as much as the aquatic treatment for tooth pain. "First, they get a branch and break it in half. Next they turn it over so that it leaks thick gunk, like drool, and they put the gunk on the tooth that hurts. Eventually it breaks into pieces, they spit them out—and no more pain!"

* * *

It's morning. Juanito is no longer howling. Victoria leaves the room, eyes on the ground. She takes the metal bowls, both now empty, to the patio, letting the weak light in through the door. A breeze moves through the house.

In the living room, Juanito and Victoria's children and in-laws are asleep, contorted into strange positions. One of their sons, Juan, wakes when his mother passes through the curtain. She tells him, "He's sleeping. His bleeding stopped."

Juan is thirty-three, and has the warmest relationship with his parents of the five children. "I was born after my dead brother," he says. "We were twins. It was a complicated birth, since it happened at home, without help." He and his siblings regret their childhood. "None of us went to school," Juan says sadly. "None of us can do much but farm. Our dad taught us that. We're teaching our children to live differently."

Outside, Victoria runs water into the bowls, but she won't be able to carry them back inside. After forty-seven years without traditional medical attention, she can hardly bend over. Her spine is wrecked, and she has chronic cardiopathy, hypertension, fibroids, and thyroid problems. "When I lived on the mountain," she says, "I worked as a seamstress and had to carry what I sewed up and down. I'd haul 110 pounds of cloth on my back, and that ruined my health. My hemoglobin got down to seven, and I decided to leave the mountain and stop being an aquatic." This was twelve years ago, and the kids feared that their parents' marriage would end when Victoria decided to seek medical help.

They all visited her during the two weeks she was hospitalized, except for Juanito. When she was released, however, he was waiting at the foot of the Sierra del Infierno to embrace her. Days later, they moved to the lowlands. "Still," she says, "I was terrified at first. I hid my pills from Juanito and took them when he wasn't around."

A rooster crows. The sun rises over a hill. Water clatters from the tap into the metal bowls. Victoria takes an old pot from the wet ground, pours corn into it, and walks through the patio, tossing food to the hungry chickens. As she sits on a tree stump to watch them eat, Juanito suddenly screams, frightening the fowl, who scatter through the yard.

THE MOCKINGBIRD

Birds sing in bird,
though we hear them in Spanish.
(Spanish is an opaque tongue full of ghost words;
bird is a transparent language with no words at all.)
—**Juan Luis Martínez,** Chilean poet

A dense mass of bodies surrounded the stage. He broke through bit by bit, wedging his shoulder into a gap, then his leg, then sucking in his stomach, dropping his head and slithering between the strangers like a snake. He said "sorry, excuse me," but no one heard him. He touched the smalls of people's backs, but few turned, and those who did looked annoyed. So many faces, so close, their features blurred by alcohol and darkness. Elbow to elbow, arms glued together by sweat, thousands swayed and chanted along with the great singer-songwriter Cándido Fabré, until their voices grew hoarse.

Periodically he paused, rose onto his toes, and tried to see if he was close, though as he approached the stage, it become harder to identify cracks in the crowd for him to wriggle through. Then he heard Fabré's raspy voice, rough with *aguardiente*, saying, "Hey! Cut it out!" The musicians stopped playing as a hole rippled through the multitude, traveling like a wave. Two men were rolling on the ground, brawling. While the guards were busy breaking up the fight, he darted past them to the stage. Once he got to the wings, he climbed the stairs and hid behind a giant speaker.

He stopped there to rest. His throat was dry. Anxiety from navigating the crowd ran through his body. He pressed his spine against the speaker, his back to the stage. His hands shook. He was sweating as if he were sitting under the midday sun, not the vanishing half-moon of dawn. He heard two men—roadies, he guessed—saying, "Fabré hasn't come to La Maya in ages. No wonder the crowd's losing their shit."

In his head, he tried to rehearse, but his thoughts rocketed away from him. He was disoriented, though not too much to watch a group of cops handcuff the wrestling men and shove them into a patrol car. He imagined himself joining them. Maybe he should get off the stage, return to the crowd, let his life continue along its course rather than risk catastrophe? He was on the verge of jumping down when the band started playing again: brass, drums, then the whole group.

In moments of uncertainty, he often pictured the tattoo on his best friend's arm: No pain, no gain. He released a long breath and walked toward the band. Thousands of faces lifted toward him.

* * *

His first performance took place in second grade. His classmates were startled by his sudden mischief: at seven, he was a solitary child who hid in the back row and had to have the words dragged from his mouth.

The teacher told him to come up to the blackboard. The other students gaped at him. Never in his life had he felt so embarrassed. "Do that again," the teacher commanded. "In front of everyone."

A moment passed. Why did I do it? he asked himself. Then he raised his right hand to his mouth, put his left hand on his small Adam's apple, and, just as he'd done before, imitated the chirp of a baby chick.

For a second time, the room burst into laughter. Not even the teacher held back. Some of his classmates shot spitballs at him. He felt like a talentless clown, a disgrace. As punishment, the teacher kept him inside during recess, a half-hour spent knocking his head gently against the wall as if it were a hammer.

His mother accompanied him to school the next morning, holding his hand. The teacher had demanded that she come. His mother asked the teacher not to add the incident to his record, promising that her son wouldn't do it again, that she'd already taken measures. "From now on, he's not allowed in the yard with the animals," she said. "He goes out there and imitates them for hours. We're done with that." No more enjoying the roosters' crows, the hens' clucks, the chicks' little cheeps in their nests. Denying him this wasn't easy for his parents, as he was happiest when he was with the animals. Otherwise, at school or at home, he retreated into himself and hardly spoke.

* * *

He was raised near a mountain on the fringes of Palma Soriano, a city in Santiago de Cuba Province. At thirty-seven, he still lives in his childhood home, a wooden shack with earthen floors, surrounded by the pastures where his parents kept the animals. He grew up among them: running barefoot, catching chickens, feeding hens and rabbits, riding the dogs and pigs like ponies. "I had to walk to school on a dangerous highway," he remembers. "Drivers would honk and shout at me because I always looked up at the birds on the wires while I walked. I liked to hear them sing. It fascinated me. Once I was listening and I guess I was on the road, not the shoulder, because I almost got hit. I remember the car—it was one of those old American ones—braking right in front of me. I dove straight into a ditch, and when the driver got out, he didn't see me at first. He must have thought I was dead, but I'd just rolled over and started running as soon as I hit the ground. I could hear him behind me, shouting, 'Little shit!'

"After that, I started going to the mountain instead of going home after school. I found an abandoned military shooting range in the forest where I could be alone. I'd spend hours there, listening to the birds, doves, mockingbirds, woodpeckers. I learned how to imitate them all. Once I was imitating a kestrel and it attacked me. It swooped down from the top of a tree, like a falcon. It probably thought I'd stolen a chick from its nest.

"Of all the birds, the mockingbird is my favorite. It's very smart. No other bird in Cuba can imitate it. It can sing more than thirty songs; I know twenty myself. I used to go on the mountain and sing to the mockingbirds and all of them would go quiet, trying to figure out what I was. I'd imagine them thinking, 'Is that the same bird as me?' Some would come out to approach me, but they flew away when they saw what I was. It's the same as if I were imitating Cándido Fabré. Fabré is Fabré. Nobody can sing like him."

* * *

In the afternoons, he would watch the older boys play baseball. Though he never missed a game, none of the boys ever noticed him. It was as if he didn't exist, as if the bleachers were empty. Still, he sat there, hoping someone would ask him to join in. He was too shy to ask.

His life was transformed the day he started singing bird songs from the stands. The other boys crowded around him, ragging on him, before asking if he wanted to join their group.

It was a trade: the boys wanted his help hunting birds on the mountain, and he wanted to make friends.

On weekends, the boys would take their slingshots to the mountain. Any bird that was captured but not wounded too badly became a pet; the rest, the ones they killed or severely injured, were sold to the Santería priests in town. The boy imposed one condition when he became part of the group: no more slingshots. You'll see, he told them.

He didn't sleep the night before his first hunting trip. He'd spent the afternoon gathering big coconut fronds and smaller leaves from castor oil plants, and he was up until dawn building cages and traps. His arsenal awed the gang. From then on, he was in charge of their expeditions. He, the invisible boy, was now the leader.

They would hunt for hours, with him guiding the pack. Although he was the youngest, nobody questioned him. He followed two strategies. One was to first identify a grove the birds liked to congregate in. There, he would hang cages baited with food on high branches and hide while he did his bird calls. The second strategy was to have the group set out traps and cages in the high grass, then lie down until the birds appeared, at which point the boys would jump out, startle them, and hope some of the flock would stumble into one of the traps.

Only the first strategy worked. So he would sing until the birds approached, saw the bread or flour or surbano leaves in the cages, and went in to eat, which made the doors close behind them. They trapped scores of birds this way. The older boys were thrilled. He, meanwhile, believed that his imitations were a gift, which he was right to exploit.

* * *

"In middle school, I brought some birds home. I loved my birds so much. I spent all my time with them: hanging out, listening, singing. My imitations reached a new level. I'd get them their breakfast, their lunch, their dinner, and after I'd fed them, I'd pull up a stool and we'd sing. But some of them started dying, and I thought it was from their sadness. My birds were in prison. I'd taken their freedom away.

"Soon the only ones left were the ones I'd gotten straight from the nest. I remember a day when an older bird died right in front of me. He'd been sad for days, not singing or eating. I was looking at him, and he just shut his eyes and opened his beak and wings. I can still see it clearly. It hurt deep in my chest. I changed after that. Birds deserve to live freely, just like us. I never went hunting again."

* * *

According to the World Wildlife Fund, poaching is the world's fourth largest illicit business, after drugs, human trafficking and forgery. In Cuba, bird smuggling is common, as we're one of the only countries whose forests, which represent 30 percent of our land, grow rather than shrink each year. Our trees hold 394 species of birds, as measured by Cuba's Center for Environmental Studies and Services; of those species, about thirty are native to the country. A man from Varadero recently got caught at the airport in Miami with two little tanagers in a Vitamin C bottle. He'd made holes in the jar so the birds could breathe, but only one survived the trip. The Border Patrol jailed him and turned his case over to the American authorities.

Juventud Rebelde, the Communist Party's youth newspaper, often reports on bird trafficking. In 2010, it covered the arrest of two men who brought sixty-two dead birds encased in formaldehyde on a train, intending to sell them to Santería practitioners. A year later, the paper followed a case in San José de las Lajas, in Mayabeque involving a man caught with sixty-five dead birds and bats in his backpack. All three men were found guilty of breaking the laws that regulate commerce in forest products and had to pay 750 pesos, or about 30 dollars. Even state outlets like *Juventud Rebelde* agree that "legislatively speaking, fauna is Cuba's least protected natural resource." No wonder the smugglers are so bold, as our laws practically give them impunity.

* * *

"My last captive was a mockingbird, who I named Fabré," he shares. "I treated that bird like my baby. I got him when he was so young that I had to teach him to eat. I'd feed him with twigs. I gave him little balls of wet flour, but I always mixed in honey or sugar, so that it was sweet. I had to open his beak for him. Sometimes I gave him orange peels and he'd take the juice drop by drop. He lived in my bedroom, and I'd cover his cage at night so that the mosquitos wouldn't bother him and he wouldn't get cold. I had to turn off lights in my room early, since he sang until he thought it was nighttime.

"I taught Fabré to sing. I did all the mockingbird calls so that he could hear what they sounded like. I made him a cassette and played it two or three times a day. After he'd learned the calls, he'd sing until dawn. He'd sing in his dreams. During the day, I'd hang his cage on the balcony, and he'd get excited. He never sat still. I'd take him to the park to play in the trees. He was like my son.

"But I wasn't a kid anymore. I had less and less time for him. Eventually I had to give him to my friend. It was so painful.

After a few weeks, I had a dream that I was sitting with him in a tree on the mountain where I found him. We were singing together. I went to visit him that day, and he didn't seem like himself, poor guy. He was sad, quiet, listless. I asked my friend what Fabré was eating, and he said flour. Fabré had never eaten just flour. A week later, he died."

* * *

What he loves most is music. Maybe that's why he's so drawn to bird song. While he was studying physical education at the Palma Soriano polytechnic school, he taught himself to play several instruments so that he could join a neighborhood band called Los Chicos de los 2000.

Cuba began the twenty-first century with a hangover. Our economy still hadn't recovered from the depression that the Soviet Union's dramatic disappearance had caused. Residents of Palma Soriano, like most Cubans, rarely had electricity. Jobs vanished and didn't return. Most families fell asleep not knowing what, or if, they would eat in the morning. Entertainment was hard to come by.

Los Chicos de los 2000 was a cure for boredom and a distraction from hunger. The band made all its instruments by hand, creating timbales out of buckets; one member improvised a conga drum with a piece of leather and a wooden box. Palma Soriano's Casa de la Cultura loaned the band a guitar to complete the conjunto. With their makeshift instruments in a wheelbarrow, the group roamed from neighborhood to neighborhood, bringing a little joy to the grateful crowds.

* * *

After graduating from school, he got a job teaching elementary school gym in La Maya, forty kilometers from his house. For fifteen years, he taught in the hot sun of Eastern Cuba, spending his days on a concrete basketball court. When he got hired, he made 150 pesos a month. When he quit in 2015, he was earning 500. During those years, his entire wardrobe consisted of two shirts, a pair of pants, and a pair of shoes—he couldn't even afford flip-flops.

* * *

It was December 22nd, which is teacher appreciation day in Cuba. His school closed at midday, and after the students left, the teachers threw a party with music, food and drinks. He didn't hold himself back from the rum, and after the party was over, on his way to the bus stop, he was amused by all the strange, inhuman faces he saw. It was as if everyone were wearing a rubber mask. "Rum," he told himself.

He started laughing out loud. Passersby kept staring at him. Rather than wait at the stop in his delicate state, he stood several meters away, doodling in the dirt with a twig. A sparrow trilled behind him. When he turned, he saw it perched on a power line. He began imitating the bird, and for the next half-hour, everyone waiting for the bus to Palma Soriano listened to him sing. As he boarded the bus, a pair of women told him, "You're better than the birds."

He spent the bus ride leaning his head on the window and thinking about the compliment. When he disembarked, he walked to a friend's house and asked him to print out photos of all the birds whose songs he could imitate. His friend made him a sandwich board that consisted of the seventeen Cuban birds whose images he had found online. The next day, he put the board over his shoulders and went out to sing in the street.

He busked from then on. He'd come home from work, ditch his briefcase full of lesson plans, drink some water, put on his sandwich board, and head out. It was fun and lucrative: he'd return home around midnight with several hundred pesos. On the weekends, he was out from morning to night, on the lookout for birthday parties, cultural activities, or just a park where he could sing. "Initially all the attention embarrassed me, but I adjusted. Really, I'm giving a concert, even if it's in the street. I had stage fright at first. But it got easier, and I started enjoying it. Besides, I was earning two or three times in a day what I made in a month at school. Crowded areas are the best, so I try to sing in parks, at parties, or at carnivals.

"I travel all over the country. I go where the money is, to places where people are happy, drunk, celebrating, ready to open their wallets. I'll go to Holguín, Pinar, Tunas, Matanzas—if there's a party, I'm there. I pack a little backpack with underwear, a clean shirt, some toiletries, and off I go.

"I travel for weeks at a time without going home. I go from carnival to carnival, sleeping outside or renting a room or singing all night. I walk around with my sign on, and someone always comes and asks me to perform. Sometimes they request specific birds, which costs extra. I sing free for children and old people. I can do that. If I'd started this job when I started teaching, I'd have bought my own house by now.

"A really bad day for me is 200 pesos. My biggest day ever, in Matanzas, was 1000. But none of this is easy. When I'm on the road, I miss my home and my family. It's tough on my body, too. I can get lightheaded from whistling. I have to take care of my lips, tongue, and teeth so that they can match the power I generate with my stomach and diaphragm. My body is my instrument.

"It's a privilege to have a job that you enjoy. I'd like to get famous. I'd like to perform on television, to have strangers ask for my autograph on the street. I'd like to get into the *Guinness Book of World Records*; to travel; to leave Cuba. I'd like to be someone, someone big, but I understand that you can only get as far in life as God lets you. It's the same with birds. You can tell from the nest which ones will grow up to sing well."

* * *

As he passed the trumpeter, the stage lights bored into his eyes. He shuddered, then slipped and stumbled. All his doubts returned as he fell, but he couldn't turn back now; so many eyes were on him. He got up and walked in front of the drummer, the guayo player, the three singers, right up to Cándido Fabré. As the security guards swung into action, he touched Fabré's shoulder and asked if he could please, please just introduce himself. With a sympathetic smile, Fabré handed him the microphone.

"I want you all to know me," he began nervously. He couldn't look out at the crowd. "My name is Riober Molina, but you can call me The Mockingbird. I'm the man who sings like a bird."

LUCK'S CHILDREN

Night is falling in Santa Clara, and at 6:50, Yasmany decides it's time to go to work. Shirtless, he rises from the curb where he's been sitting with his friends following their pickup soccer game. He goes into his house, where the phone rings continuously. (It won't shut up until 8:00.) He walks through the living room, down a long, narrow hallway with two adjoining bedrooms, into the kitchen, which is at the back of the house.

Yasmany sits down at the table. His mother, leaning on the counter, lights a cigarette and trains her eyes on the nape of her son's neck, watching everything that he writes down. With a cell phone in one hand and a calculator in the other, Yasmany races through the day's accounts, driving his blue ballpoint into the page. He writes without looking, like a soccer coach, but instead of players he has his calculator and countless scraps of paper. Occasionally he checks the time on his phone.

A visibly drunk man appears at the back door. Very quietly and seriously, he gives Yasmany a list of numbers and a five-peso bill. A teenage boy, wearing only frayed, ratty shorts, shows up with a list that he says belongs to his grandmother. A neighbor pops by and asks Yasmany how he can still be doing his accounts so late in the evening. It's only 7:18, Yasmany answers; he's got more than enough time to finish by 7:55.

A few minutes later, Yasmany gets up from the table and changes into a numberless F.C. Barcelona jersey without showering away the sweat from the soccer game. At 7:32, he tucks the many lists he has accumulated and a wad of cash into a small black fanny pack he fastens across his chest. He gets on his bike and rides off in sandals, chewing on his pen.

At 8:00, the evening's winning *La Bolita* numbers will be announced, and before that happens, Yasmany has to deliver all of the illegal money he's collected today.

* * *

In his celebrated 1832 treatise, *Memoir on Vagrancy in Cuba*, José Antonio Saco wrote that, "[n]o city, town, or corner is free from [the] devouring cancer," of gambling. "It has crept from Punta de Maisí to Cabo de San Antonio, from the westernmost tip of the island to the east." In Cuba today, the law threatens any "banker, messenger, collector, or promoter of illegal gambling" with "one to three years in prison, payments of 300 to 1000 pesos, or both," adding that "if the aforementioned crimes are committed by two or more people or involve minors under sixteen years of age, the prison term will be three to eight years." Despite these harsh penalties, more Cubans play *La Bolita* than baseball, the national sport.

In the twentieth century, when Cuba became a neocolonial property of the United States, gambling on the island was run by men who sold small, numbered balls called *bolitas*, hence the name of the game. A ball cost anywhere from a cent to a peso. The winning numbers were announced on the radio or, later, on public-access television. Unlike the more expensive state lottery, even the poorest citizens could afford to play *La Bolita*.

When Fidel Castro came to power in 1959, his government concentrated on the ills of Cuban society. Gambling was among his first targets, but rather than stop it, Castro's policies turned *La Bolita* into an underground criminal enterprise.

* * *

Also called *Charada Cubana*, *La Bolita* is essentially the same as the Pick 3 and Pick 4 lotteries common in Florida and much of Latin America. At midday and again in the evening, an air cannon randomly shoots out three numbers from 0 to 100. You win by having guessed the lucky combination before it's announced. You can bet as much or little as you like, and if you win, the game's organizers multiply what you put in. Gamblers learn the day's results in one of three ways: by listening to a shortwave radio station that broadcasts from Miami; watching illegal international satellite channels; or subscribing to a new Android app that messages you the winning numbers, which costs the equivalent of $3 a month in pesos.

The game's administrators have created such ingenious and effective underground networks that it's almost like a drug cartel. At the top are the bankers. They pay the daily winners, maintain a cadre of salaried employees, and hold onto the money that's left over after the payouts. Few people know anything about them: their names, their collection strategies, their investments. "Bankers only trust their families," Yasmany says. "It's too risky to let anybody else count or touch the money. In this business, it's easy to get ripped off."

At the next level are the messengers, who bring the day's cash to the bankers and are the only ones trusted with their identities. Under the messengers are the collectors, who are the public face of the game. They go door to door in their neighborhoods—or, more riskily, let the gamblers come to their door—collecting bets. Yasmany is a collector and a messenger.

* * *

On a rainy afternoon in a café high in the hills of Santa Clara's Parque Vidal, surrounded by his friends, Yasmany tells me that he used to work as a municipal groundskeeper for the city. "I was a janitor for a while, too," he says. "But then life got complicated, and I had to come up with other ways of earning. Official salaries are useless. I started this job, and then my son was born, and I kept going to support him and my wife."

Yasmany got involved with *La Bolita* twelve years ago. Today, at age thirty-two, his life is dedicated to the game. His earnings and winnings go toward building a small house near his mother's (it's still under construction), saving up to go to Panama or other countries that don't require Cubans to get tourist visas, and to purchase wholesale clothing he can resell at a markup.

Yasmany is such a hardcore soccer fan that he named his son Messi. He tells me a story about how he once got in trouble for Messi's sake: "Some plainclothes cops started following me. I took off running, and I'd have gotten away, but I dropped some lists and Messi's tablet, which had photos of him on it. I went to pick it up, and the cops grabbed me. But I told them I just played *Charada*, and since I didn't have cash on me or in my house, I didn't get charged with anything."

We're standing on the café's terrace, our elbows on the railing. Blackbirds circle, cawing, then land in the trees as Yasmany tells me that he never keeps *La Bolita* money in his house. "At home, I never have more than $10, so if the cops come, I can't get in trouble."

As the afternoon retreats, the dull gray clouds give way to thunderheads. The winning numbers are announced at 2:00 and 8:00, which means that Yasmany has to deliver all the lists and bets he's collected by 1:55, then again by 7:55: "I have to get there before the balls come out so that nobody cheats or bets after hearing the results. If I'm late, the banker won't let me in. It's a big responsibility. Imagine if I was late and somebody whose list I had won. I'd be in deep shit."

Most of the collectors in Santa Clara ride bicycles or scooters to collect their bets. This helps them to avoid attracting police attention. "If you don't walk," Yasmany says, "no one notices you." For collectors who aren't also messengers, it also helps to constantly change delivery spots: "We choose the delivery spot the day before. It's always somewhere out of the way, and we never repeat it. In twelve years, I've never gone back to the same place twice."

Yasmany tries to avoid his own neighborhood before drop time. As we head there, he tells me that "we've got too many tattletales around here, so I have to be careful." When he's not home, his mother and brother collect the bets.

* * *

Yasmany and I settle on the curb outside his house. A neighbor comes by and shows Yasmany a list and some bills—I can't see the denominations—and Yasmany, annoyed, tells him to leave it in the house. An old woman then approaches with a list and ten pesos, and Yasmany, with a gorgeous sleight of hand, accepts both without seeming to see her at all. One hand gives; the other hand takes. No looks, no conversation, nothing.

You can tell the hour is approaching. Energy swirls through the streets. Out of superstition, most gamblers rarely bet before the very last moment, and now they stream into Yasmany's house. We remain outside on the curb. An elegantly dressed older man comes out of the house, nodding to signal that he made his bet. Inside, the phone rings and rings. An older woman in a red Soviet sedan pulls over and shamelessly asks the men gathered around us which numbers to play. Somebody tells her some combination, and she nods and drives away without placing a bet. A medical student goes in the house, white coat draped over his arm. A housewife walks up holding a dish towel from which she removes a scrap of lined paper and a three-peso bill with Che Guevara on it. "Not all my clients come here," Yasmany says. "I also collect from the houses that are on the way to the banker. I write down everyone's name and numbers so that I can verify who won. Otherwise, the banker could screw me." We're sitting under a streetlight, and in its glow, I can see that his palms are stained blue with the ink he uses to compile his master list.

* * *

Norberto speaks to me as if I were a number, as if the world and its inhabitants were a complex yet solvable equation. He's a seventy-year-old retired high-school physics teacher who started playing *Charada* when he was seven. He's white, of Spanish descent, and obese. He wears sunglasses and a straw hat to shield his eyes from the sun, since he just had cataract surgery.

Norberto plays religiously, never skipping a day. Sitting in a wooden armchair in his living room, he tells me that the game originated with Cuba's Chinese immigrants, but their version only used the numbers one to thirty-six. Next came Dominican *Charada*, which goes up to one-hundred. Cuban players use one of three strategies to try and win: choosing numbers in order; relying on omens and dreams; and maintaining data and statistics on which numbers are the luckiest over time.

Norbeto interrupts our interview to pick-up yesterday's winnings and deliver his daily bet. He's playing eighty-nine and three today. Eighty-nine, he says, represents the lottery in the numerological system that gives each digit a particular meaning. As for three, that's the number on the left sleeve of my sweatshirt. "Some people listen to clairvoyants who do more complicated numerology with Bible verses," he says. "Before, the numbers just had one meaning each, but the game's evolved a lot since then."

Although Norberto is consumed by *Charada*, he's also clear-eyed about its implications. "You have to be tough," he says. "You can't let the game play you. I separate my living expenses, and that money, I never touch."

He tells me he once had a dream about a hen and her yellow chicks. When he left his house that morning, the streets were full of people in yellow sweaters. He then ran into a fellow gambler and told him about the dream: the gambler told him that the number one represents baby chicks. Later, it started raining and while sheltering under an awning, Norberto saw a truck full of sunflowers with a one painted on its side. When he arrived at the collector's house, he met a man who always played one, but said he was skipping the number that day. Norberto counted the chicks in his dream—nine—and put ten pesos on nine and one. The following morning, he gathered his winnings: 13,000 pesos. "A high point," he says. But after such highs comes an obsession with victory that can easily grow dark. "You have to look out for that."

Norberto illustrates this warning by telling me about a friend of his, a hotel manager in Quemado de Güines whose numbers would always hit. One day, he had no idea which numbers to play, so he put 500 pesos on his house number, and won several thousand pesos. But after that, he had a losing streak. He started selling his valuables and stealing from the hotel to finance his habit, racking up a debt of 300,000 pesos. He went to a loan shark, which made matters worse. He eventually lost his house, his cars and his wife, who took their two children to live in Eastern Cuba. An audit at the hotel later uncovered the embezzled money, and he ended up in prison for four years.

"See?" Norberto concludes. "Money can suck you in."

* * *

"I do 200 pesos a day," Omar explains. "Before I played by omens, but I switched to statistics. Dreams are good, but only the week you have them."

It took me several days for me to get Omar, a baker, to answer his door, and when he finally did, his eyes were crusty with sleep. He's Black, and has yellow, plaque-coated teeth. His house is near the monument commemorating Che Guevara's capture of an armored train in 1958, and we talk in a park with a view of the statue. The park has three swings, a metal roundabout, and play structures so ancient they could only survive in Cuba. Not a single child is in sight.

"If I hit it big, I'll rent a bus and invite the whole neighborhood to the beach or a hotel pool," Omar tells me, waving his hands excitedly. He then relates a famous local tale: "Some Venezuelan reporters were shooting a segment with Chávez and Castro in the main plaza of Santa Clara. Chávez said that he was going to play sixty-six that day because it was his dad's lucky number, but then he found out that gambling wasn't legal here and had to apologize.

"I started playing *La Bolita* in the nineties, but my dad was in the Party, so I had to hide it," Omar says. His arms are ashy, and he's wearing shorts and sandals. His legs knock together in the cold wind. "I never stopped, though. I've had times when I bet 50 cents and times when I bet 500 pesos. Right now, I'm

15,000 pesos in debt. It's an addiction. I have an angel on one shoulder telling me to quit and a devil on the other telling me I can win."

Omar is married to a doctor. She's an international aid worker in Venezuela, and has been gone for three years. She's earned enough to renovate their house, but she doesn't know that Omar has sold most of their possessions—their DVD player, television, washing machine and half the living-room furniture—because of his gambling. In tears, he says, "She's coming to visit soon, and I'm going to try to get it all back by then."

Omar has had unlucky streaks before. One time, when he had no money or food, in desperation he sought out a local fortune teller, an elderly lady. She told him, "In Da Vinci's Last Supper, there's a man no one notices. He's the Señor del Buen Despacho. Put out a glass of water and an unlit candle, choose your numbers, and tell him you'll light the candle if you win."

Omar obeyed the fortune teller, and that afternoon, while he was showering, a neighbor called through the window to tell him that his number had come up. Omar bounded naked from the bathroom, covered in soap, to light the candle.

* * *

Yasmany isn't feeling well today. He was kept up all night by stomach cramps, and can hardly get out of bed. But his work is seven days a week, with no vacation or sick time, so his brother Pancho fills in. Pancho used to do collections himself, but he got out of the game years ago. Still, the gamblers know and trust him.

Pancho gets on Yasmany's bicycle and heads toward Camacho. However, the neighborhood is inaccessible today:

there's fumigation happening, and the chief of police is there. So he heads instead to La Candonga, an area full of state-sanctioned private businesses selling food and miscellaneous goods. Here, the gamblers gather their lists together in one store to help the collector. Pancho enters through the back door. He gets out his phone and tallies the accounts while leaning against the door jamb. When he is done, he tucks the lists in his brother's black fanny pack and is gone, quick as a shooting star.

His last collection is at the local primary school. Unlike his brother, Pancho hates this place—he says that he feels exposed here. He has to park his bicycle, go inside the building, dodge the bust of Cuba's apostle, José Martí, and let the teacher know he's in the hallway, waiting for her. She tells her students to sit tight and leaves them alone in the classroom so that she can place her bet.

* * *

The living room has two dolls on display: a white one dressed in yellow clothes, and a Black one dressed in blue. These are the orishas, Oshún and Yemayá. Above them is a shelf holding a statuette of the Virgen de la Caridad; a bottle of Soroa wine; a can of Cristal beer; and the flags of Argentina, Spain and F.C. Barcelona. There are two religions in this house: Santería and soccer.

Yasmany's stomach has improved, so he's helping his uncles and Pancho build a new staircase. Reggaeton blasts from a bedroom, so loud it rattles the wheelbarrows of cement, gravel and stone dust. Bottles of rum accumulate on the ground.

In the *Charada* system, twenty-three represents stairs. Somebody needs a knife, and the one he is given has a twenty-three-gauge blade. Yasmany looks at the time: 7:23. "Lots of signs," he says. "I better play."

He gathers his lists, and gets ready. All activity in the house ceases. Everyone studies Yasmany as he sits at the table. A yellow bulb swings from a cobwebby wire above him, illuminating the cement splattered on his limbs. The phone rings mercilessly. A woman comes by to plead for a free number. She'll pay tomorrow, she swears.

At 7:33, Yasmany gets up. He grabs a hat, a sweatshirt, his bag, and walks his bike to the door. Before he leaves, he calls to his mother, "Don't forget to record Messi's cartoons."

MUD

José is eighty-nine, and he knows where everything is. Everything he needs, anyway. He knows that beside his bed is a prehistoric fan that still does its best to move air, and he knows that beside the fan on his scratched, scarred nightstand is his loyal squire: an old radio. He also knows that when he gets out of bed, his feet will sink into mud riddled with crab holes.

José can't see his dark, soapy limbs when he washes in the water he heats in a small metal pot on his hot plate. He cooks, scrubs, and dries by touch alone. José lives by himself in El Fanguito, one of Havana's poorest neighborhoods. He's lucky he can't look at it.

* * *

Jammed against the elegant Vedado neighborhood, El Fanguito is an island within the city, an isolated community that outsiders rarely visit. You'd have no reason to go there unless you wanted to see for yourself how polluted the Río Almendares is or catch the local group, Charanga Habanera, playing a Monday show.

El Fanguito has one street, though that's putting it generously. Calle 30 is less a part of the neighborhood than its limit, cutting it off from Vedado. Outside Calle 30 is city, smoke, action; inside is the stench of the river and not much else. El Fanguito is a labyrinth of false starts and dead ends, huts slouching together, rotten planks kissing corroded zinc. Occasionally you might spot a fortunate family's stucco house. If El Fanguito were a model, you could scoop it up in one hand and crush it.

* * *

In 2009, José's left eye started failing, his vision deteriorating into blurry images and indistinct gray silhouettes. He had a cataract, which required immediate surgery. Six months later, the story repeated itself in his other eye.

His doctor prescribed complete rest after the operations, but José's only companion was a calico cat who couldn't help him carry water indoors in a twenty-liter plastic tank or haul a crate of beans, rice and brown and white sugar home from a bodega. When the hurricanes came during José's recovery, the cat couldn't help him brace his collapsing home against the winds. He evacuated to a shelter with his neighbors, then returned to a house that no longer had a roof. He had to haul beams up a ladder himself to replace it.

However, it was José's solitude, not his poverty, that cost him his sight. "My wife and son got sick of living with an old man and left for Santiago," he says reproachfully, refusing to go into any more detail about their departure.

In the thirty-three years that José has lived in El Fanguito, the houses have always abutted one another—privacy isn't part of life here. Only the few freestanding stucco houses in the neighborhood are exempt from the reggaeton and folk music that thump through the other homes' wooden walls and into your head.

Nearly all the houses are shanties, cobbled together with the ingenuity of need. Communities like this are precarity made visible. Most shantytown dwellers are migrants from other provinces who came to Havana hoping for easier lives and instead got a few square meters of mud and just enough roof to hide the stars at night. "I built my house twenty-eight years ago," José tells me. "It took two months and a day. I had a construction job then, and I could gather stuff at work." When José says "gather," he means steal. Cubans call this sort of theft *la lucha*: the struggle. Official salaries don't stretch far enough to provide a dignified life, and so for most Cubans, their jobs are important primarily for what they can "gather" from them.

And so this was how José got his home, a shadowy cave without electricity, illuminated only in the mornings and afternoons when the sun insinuates itself through the cracks in the decrepit walls and roof, highlighting what José can no longer see: the mold on his mattress, the junk accruing on the muddy ground and the tarps he drapes everywhere in an unsuccessful attempt to shield the house from the rain that pours mercilessly in, ruining his belongings and leaving behind the stench of decay when it stops.

* * *

José's house faces a landfill, a green patch of weeds where sheep graze when the families without plumbing aren't there emptying the crates and bags they use as toilets. Better to toss their waste in the grass than the already-contaminated Almendares, where children swim on weekend afternoons. "A boy died of an infection from the river recently," Nilda tells me. "He went swimming with a cut on his foot. He lasted less than three days in the hospital."

Nilda is fifty, mixed-race, warm and spiritual. She wears images of the orishas Oshún and Obatalá around her neck. She's part of a big Fanguito family and is sort of the unofficial mayor of the neighborhood. She was the local delegate to the National Assembly from 2005 to 2009, and the residents still congregate together outside her house at all hours, perching on a big ceiba tree's roots or sitting on the ground by her plastic chair to chat. "Our conditions here are very precarious," she explains. "Most of the adults have no income except for their pensions. We used to get donations from the government, but that stopped. Now, no one comes to see if we're eating or how we're getting by. It doesn't matter to them if the river ruins our lives."

According to the 2005 census, El Fanguito contained 199 homes, only one of which was legal. As a result, the latest census, taken in 2012, didn't include the neighborhood. "We aren't typical," Nilda says. "We don't own our homes, and the state says that our living here isn't permanent, so we can't buy the land. But we still get bills for our water, gas and electricity, no matter how temporary we are. We're like refugees. It's been this way since the Revolution."

El Fanguito's density has risen significantly since 2005. At the same time, its inhabitants' conditions remain abysmal, not that the state seems to care. Decades ago, the municipal government created a bit of hope by offering subsidies for the residents to construct apartment towers in neighboring Vedado. It took twenty years to build them; in the end, 110 people managed to escape El Fanguito. "Symbolically," Nilda says, "it was huge to see our neighbors building something of their own. But in practice, it didn't change much. All the families here had grown so much that everyone who moved to Vedado had to leave relatives behind, in the same bad conditions."

Real change appeared to be happening in 2007, when Carlos Lage, an economic reformer who was then Cuba's vice president, spearheaded something called the Fanguito Project. The goals of the project were to restore and beautify the area, donate construction materials to families in need and clean up the Almendares. Initially, Nilda says, the idea was to "get us some infrastructure:" pave the streets, partition vacant lots, and, most urgently, build an esplanade on the ravaged riverbank to separate the houses from the water. The government also planned to put in little parks with benches and fruit trees, small versions of Havana's central Parque Metropolitano, and piers and dry docks for community members' boats.

But then Fidel Castro got sick and handed the reins to his brother Raúl, who, in 2009, reshuffled the government, dismissing many high-level politicians. Among those let go were Lage and his fellow reformer, Felipe Pérez Roque, the foreign minister. Raúl Castro, in one of the "reflections" he published in the state press, wrote of Lage and Pérez Roque that the "honey of the power for which they had known no sacrifice awoke in them ambitions that led them to an unworthy role." His accusations weren't true, but that didn't make them any less of a kick in the teeth for El Fanguito. "After Lage left," Nilda says, "it all fell apart. No one took an interest after that. I quit the government."

Despite the years of neglect from the state, Nilda and her neighbors still try to do what they can. For example, they have repeatedly gotten arrested for building cinderblock walls around the landfill. "We tried requesting the land from the Institute of Physical Planning," she says, "but nobody responded. Eventually we decided to do it without permission, but any time we get going, the cops show up."

* * *

When the Almendares crests, it floods the neighborhood. When it recedes, it leaves so much mud in its wake that the shantytown turns into a swamp. Sometimes the water is as high as a grown man's knees. Children can't go to school on those days, though if the flooding isn't too catastrophic, they roll up their pants, balance their backpacks on their heads, stuff rags in their pockets to clean themselves off, and trudge barefoot through the mud.

A state resolution that appeared in *La Gaceta de Cuba* in 2014 announced that the government would concentrate on citizens living in flood plains when carrying out its housing program. It has not been followed. "After the resolution," Nilda tells me angrily, "we asked Physical Planning to help us, and nothing. We still can't even get construction subsidies because we don't legally own our homes."

Like a good daughter of Oshún, the goddess of water, Nilda lived beside the river for a long time. But then she got sick of the Almendares rushing into her home. "Before," she says, "the water didn't rise this much. But starting a couple years ago, the river floods constantly and comes higher and higher all the time. It's terrifying how routine it became. Nighttime was the scariest. We'd see crocodiles and huge walking catfish. I'd rather sleep outside than be surrounded by that." She adds that, "In my new house, I get wet from above, not below." This is because Nilda's new home is like an old convertible: it doesn't have a roof.

* * *

Almost no one in El Fanguito has a formal job, so its residents spend much of their time walking around or sitting outside on what passes for curbs. Young people raise pigeons, the shantytown's national sport, on their roofs. Stray dogs roam the streets.

A major problem in the neighborhood is the lack of gas. The people who live in houses without gas lines use a thirty-pound metal gas tank called a *balita*. Renting a *balita* costs 400 pesos a month; the gallon of gas it holds costs an additional 120. On average, a Fanguito family has ten members occupying three or four little huts, which is too much for a single *balita* to serve, so, Nilda says that "they buy *balitas* illegally or from people who live alone and need the money. Almost everyone cooks with kerosene or hot plates, but kerosene is very dangerous here. Our houses are so close together that if one person's kerosene splashes, the whole street can go up in flames."

José is one of those who sells his *balita* to other families, trading a gas flame for the weak heat of a hot plate. He receives 192 pesos, or $8.00, which augments his meager pension.

He hasn't heard from the government in a year, since a few members of the Social Security staff came by and talked to him about his situation, telling him that he qualified for a construction subsidy and daily assistance at home. Neither came through. "I did get something from them two months ago," he corrects. "Ten bottles of dish soap and three bars of shower soap."

* * *

At the Social Security bureau office that handles El Fanguito, 56 of the 90 desks are occupied. Each employee has more than 2,000 clients, none of whom get a visit from their social worker more than four times a year. "All our constituents matter," says Yaima Fáez, who runs the department that assists those who receive a too-small pension—or no pension at all. "We can't rank their need. What we can do is ensure that our clients have beds, mattresses, cribs, sheets, clothes and shoes."

Legally, a social worker can have no more than 600 clients, but the lack of personnel makes that impossible. Yaima blames "their salaries, which are miniscule: 335 pesos a month"—$14.00. "Between that and their unmanageable workloads," she says, "it's no wonder most quit after three or four months."

* * *

Once a day, José is able to drink cold water: at lunch, when, cane in hand, he navigates the puddles and potholes to get to the state-run El Río cafeteria.

El Río is furnished with four iron tables, each of which has four chairs. The place also has a television. It's steamy inside with the day's heat and the smoke coming from the kitchen, where giant pots sit on open flames. For a decade, the cafeteria has fed lunch and dinner to 51 seniors from El Fanguito, 20 of whom are registered for food assistance, which means that their meals cost 20 cents a visit. All the rest pay one peso. "We got a new administrator who really improved the food," José tells me. "Before, our meals had no fat. We got heaps of steamed vegetables, or salted and boiled. If we had chicken, it was just chopped-up bits of meat and bones. Once, on a holiday, the old administrator stole both the pigs we'd been given. I know we're all struggling, but take a portion, a leg, not two pigs."

El Río's clients begin complaining the moment they arrive, generating an endless din. José pours his cold water into a ceramic cup, nibbles a tasteless slice of bread, and then eats the rest of his meal.

* * *

After lunch, José heads outside. Despite his poor vision, he never stumbles—he knows the uneven sidewalks, the tilted lampposts, the dumpsters that spill trash in his way. "I've never fallen," he says. "And I've never had help. I have my cane from the church to guide me." He even walks by himself to pick up his pension from the bank at the corner of Avenida Paseo and Línea, two kilometers from his home.

José's main "entertainment" is catching crabs in his house. In El Fanguito, you only have to dig thirty or so centimeters down to touch water, which is ideal crab territory. There are burrows all over the neighborhood, including in the hard mud of José's floor. He listens to their scratching claws, then goes after them with a broom. "My crabs put on concerts if I don't shut them up. One time I had a dent in my house bigger than my foot. Before I leveled the ground, I boiled a pot of water and dumped it in, and not another crab came out of there."

Against the rats, he has his cat, Misun, to defend him. "She won't let them touch me. She hunts like a vampire at night. In the day, she wants to leave the house with me, but I'm scared to let her. Too many dogs around here."

* * *

José keeps two keys in a red pouch around his neck: one for his regular house lock, the other for the rusty padlock he uses on the door for extra security. Still, he asks, "Who's going to rob me?"

Though José's exhausted hands struggle with the padlock whenever he is leaving—or returning—home, using it reminds him that his home does in fact exist, despite what the government census says.

THE HUNTER

It was a rainy afternoon in Viñales, and Ernesto had the Italian woman naked on the kitchen counter in her rental house when his iPhone started to vibrate. It was the French woman calling.

Earlier, following lunch, Ernesto had come up behind the Italian woman as she washed the dishes, pressed his bare, muscular torso to her back, and softly kissed her neck and shoulders, then turned her around and undressed her. He'd completely forgotten about the French woman, who'd emailed the previous day, saying she'd arrive in the morning and had arranged to introduce him to her Cuban relatives that afternoon.

Ernesto made an excuse and left the overexcited Italian woman on the counter. He went into the bathroom, and answered his phone, "*Salut, mon amour. Est-ce que tu est arrive bien*?"

"I made it, *mon amour*. When are you coming to Havana?"

"*Aujourd'hui, ma chérie*."

It was the Italian woman' s last day in Cuba, which was a problem.

Ernesto returned from the bathroom and, as if nothing had happened, knelt and kissed his way from the Italian woman's feet up to her face.

He'd already had sex with her three times that day. After round four, he said, "My sister called. My mom's sick again. I have to go to Baracoa." It was two in the afternoon, and Ernesto was drained and slick with sweat. The Italian woman stretched out among the knives and frying pans, as if the counter were a waterbed.

* * *

Ernesto and I first met in Guanabo, a resort town east of Havana. The town has rough, hard beaches, but we were at a house with a pool, which had been rented by the mother-in-law of a friend of Ernesto's. She's Cuban, married to a French Congolese man; they split their time between the Republic of the Congo, France and Miami, but she comes home once a year to Cuba to see her daughters and mother. Her husband's niece, Fadih, was the French woman who had called Ernesto.

Fadih was born in Brazzaville. She's thirty-three and weighs nearly 300 pounds. She wears glasses and has very dark skin. She and Ernesto had met four months before the phone call, while she was in Havana for her cousin's wedding. "I snagged Fadih at the airport," Ernesto told me by the pool. "I'd just dropped a Spanish girl off there. Fadih had never visited Cuba before, and the second she walks out the door, here I am. A sign, right?" He interrupts our conversation to get up and dive elegantly into the water in his tight, highlighter-yellow trunks.

Fadih's visit was supposed to just be for the wedding. Instead, she spent two months on the island after bumping into Ernesto at door four in arrivals at José Martí Airport. "I saw her looking around, all confused, and bam! Got her address, got her number, got my game face on," Ernesto continues after he gets out of the pool. He called her every night, and loitered around her relatives' building until she appeared. One day, he invited her to join him on the Malecón (a long seawall that runs along the coast of Havana which is a popular destination for locals and tourists). She drank beer; he drank juice. "I lucked out," he says triumphantly. "None of my other girls were there, so all I had to do was bag her." And bag her he did. She changed her airline ticket and let him show her around Cuba. After visiting cities and beaches all over the island, he brought her to Baracoa, in Guantánamo Province, to introduce her to his mother. "Bringing her home was a good move, but I know the drill with foreigners. I give them pretty Cuba, pretty me. Baracoa was about convincing her that I wasn't just playing, that I was in it for real."

* * *

When the USSR disintegrated in the early 1990s, Cuba went into an economic freefall. Without the handouts from the former Soviet Union, the Cuban economy cratered. GDP contracted by 36 percent, and the crisis ate up the welfare programs that the Revolution had created. This crash reverberated throughout society. For example, between 1990 and 1995, the average adult Cuban lost between 5 to 25 percent of their body weight, according to state economic studies. Fidel Castro called this time the "Special Period." Survival became difficult, and once clandestine ways of earning a living, such as prostitution, burst out into the open. As the government turned its back on the populace, the modern Cuban hustler was born.

Ernesto's family barely made it through the Special Period. His father had died of a heart attack when he was eleven, and after his mother lost her state job in one of the massive layoffs, Ernesto had no choice: he had to earn a living. He quit school at fourteen and joined a gaggle of local teens who spent their days in the center of Baracoa, hustling for money from tourists.

Ernesto didn't tell his mother what he was doing. Instead, he let her continue waking him at 6:30 a.m., dressing him in his pioneer uniform with its red bandanna, and putting his stuff in his backpack, which he hid, along with his white shirt and scarf, in a crumbling, abandoned house. Unburdened, he'd head to the hotel district in historic Baracoa and get to work. "Mami didn't guess until I gave her a whole crate of ham and cheese and soda, and some American coins, and there's only one way I could've gotten those. But what was she going to say? If I hadn't started bringing home food, we'd have died of hunger," Ernesto says, not laughing. I've never seen him this serious.

* * *

Ernesto graduated from scavenging gum and sandwiches from tour buses to recommending restaurants in the historic center, in the process earning commissions from the proprietors. Instead of begging for American coins, he sold Cuban currency, highlighting Che and José Martí's portraits on the bills. But he was still just scraping by. He saw only one way to earn real money: seducing foreign women. "Foreigners come here for us," he told me by the pool in Guanabo, his back to Fadih's Cuban cousins. "It's the truth."

He started having breakfast in hotels and fancy tourist cafés, but that ended up draining his savings. "It wasn't the right energy," he says. "I wasn't going to get their attention unless I looked Cuban: rum in my hand, hips moving, whistling at them. And that's not the cafés. It's night, in a club." He started exercising and claiming he was in college, studying physical education. "No one wants a moron, man," he tells me. "I'm hot, I've got the build, I'm the right color for them, but that's not enough. I read the paper, put the news on. Women like it when I talk to them about the world."

* * *

During the Special Period, many poor Cubans began to see tourists as goldmines. To them, one visitor to the island was a steady income; a group, a business. Castro tried to stifle this budding industry by banning Cuban citizens from hotels and tourist attractions, an infantilizing, authoritarian reaction, like sending your child upstairs when you have guests. It thus became challenging for Cubans to meet foreigners. It wasn't until 2008 that Raúl Castro relaxed the laws.

Now, anywhere you go on the island, you see couples, one Cuban and one not, who are obviously sustained by practicality rather than love; couples that you can immediately tell are together because one likes the other's wallet. Maybe it's a stylish older woman holding hands with a charismatic Black man in his twenties, a muscular guy, probably a good dancer, with dreads or braids; maybe it's a gray-haired man blowing cigar smoke at a slim brown girl with long curls and full lips. These hustlers congregate in tourist areas and at the chic bars that are popping up around the island. Charm and Cuban stereotype are their bait; foreigners swim around them, eager to swallow the hook.

* * *

Ernesto is a nomad. He drifts from Eastern to Western Cuba, hotel to hotel, rental to rental. If he's in a private home, it likely belongs to friends of his clients. If he's anywhere else, the client is paying. He religiously sends much of the money he earns to his mother in Baracoa, never skipping a month. She's sixty-six and strong as a draft horse, and invests the cash in her coconut-candy business.

Still, Ernesto hasn't been home to Baracoa in over a year. He says he won't return until it's time to say his farewells when he's leaving Cuba for good. He can't stand living in poverty anymore.

* * *

A month after we met in Guanabo, Ernesto told me he was in Havana, and we met at Café Maimanés, in Vedado. Fadih was in Paris. He'd just come from Varadero, where he'd said goodbye to a woman named Judith, who was flying back to Germany; in the morning, he was picking up an English woman at the airport. He said that he planned to spend the night alone in a rented room in Miramar, an upscale Havana neighborhood, then collect the Brit and take her to the same hotel in Varadero that he'd left with Judith less than twenty-four hours before.

"I'm a professional," Ernesto tells me, smiling. "I've got tons of competition, so I have to focus. Set myself apart. Stay in shape. I'm not vegetarian, but I mostly eat greens. I don't eat fat or drink beer. Rum, whisky, beer only if I really have to and the girl's worth it. But I don't swallow. I just kiss the glass, get some foam on my lip so that the girl can taste it."

When Ernesto isn't busy with his clients, he's at the gym. He prefers planks, pull-ups and bars to lifting weights. He does lots of abs, and he runs, but not too far; he can't risk getting scrawny. At thirty-four, he looks like a gymnast, all streamlined muscle, a body designed to appeal to all sorts of women: white, Black, Latina, Asian, short, fat, thin, tall. He's at your service, up for anything, a mannequin on constant display.

When Ernesto catches a woman's eye, it means he gets free dinners, beach days, nights in air-conditioned rooms. It means commissions from the hotels and restaurants he takes her to. It means selling her marked-up rum or tobacco. And at the end of her trip, it means taking home some items or clothes. All very subtle, but it's business, and the women are generally well-aware of what's going on. "We don't have to discuss it," he says. "No contract. Usually, the girls get it, though some poor things don't see the bill coming till it's time."

Sometimes his payment is a pair of flip-flops. Sometimes, an iPhone. Donations, tax-free. And if the client's content with the services rendered, if the affair is steamy enough to continue online, then who knows? All Ernesto's efforts could end in a wedding and a new life. In any country. He doesn't care which one.

* * *

Ernesto's body is perfectly chiseled. His skin is brown, his eyes slanted. His curls brush his solid shoulders. On the left side of his six-pack is a knife scar from a prison fight.

He says he last ate bread fifteen years ago, and now he feels sick at the sight of it. "I haven't touched that shit since jail. I did three years for prostitution and harassing tourists"—both illegal in Cuba. He was incarcerated in Santiago's Boniato Prison, melting in his narrow cell in the summer, missing the sunlight in the damp winter. "I wasn't scared of the cops in Baracoa. I knew them and they knew me. But I got cocky. I was coming out of a club with a Brazilian girl who was wild for me, really nuts, and the pigs grabbed me and tossed me in the car without a word. Judge, jury and three years, bang! I lost the Brazilian girl. I was living with bad guys, man, really bad guys, and I was only twenty-one when I went in. I got this scar fighting two guys who wanted to rape me. I had to get tough."

"And you didn't learn your lesson?" I ask.

"Man, you're looking at it the wrong way. I came out of there stronger, more focused, ready to grab every girl who might get me out of this piece-of-shit country someday."

* * *

Ernesto ended up ditching the Italian woman in Viñales. "She was leaving anyway, and we were just partying. She wasn't going to marry me. She's not my ticket out of here."

He then headed to Guanabo, where Fadih and her family were waiting. In front of their house, he got nervous, as this was a Cuban family, not his usual audience. "Cubans can spot a hustler, but who cares? No fear in here," he told me, thumping his chest. "I've just got to show them that I'm a catch."

Fadih's family couldn't believe she hadn't picked up on his game. "I overheard her aunt saying, 'If she gets him out of Cuba, he'll disappear the first time he goes for a walk.'"

However, her cousin defended him, "So what, Ma? Where's she going to get another guy that hot?"

Fadih's face was radiant with pleasure. Ernesto whispered in her ear, and she smiled and caressed his neck. Her relatives stared at him, incredulous, as he ate, talked to Fadih, dove in the pool. "Sure, they're protective. Any Cuban would be. But I'm not scared. I didn't get into this game yesterday. I'm good at my job, and that's what matters. I've got that girl in love with me."

* * *

During our conversations, Ernesto never sets his phone down. He's got a ton of contacts. "All this is from years of work," he tells me, holding up his iPhone to show me the female faces in his WhatsApp chat. "And it takes work still. I sit down with my email, Facebook, calendar, check dates so that my girls don't overlap. I don't hunt for more. I've got mine. I don't need to compete. I'm good.

"It was hard at the beginning because I was shy, but you can't stay shy in this game. What you do is, you attack with your eyes. It gives you a starting point. If a woman really looks at you, or if she looks away and then right back, you've got her. Easy. Write that down. After that, it's just chatting, inviting her out, getting ahead with her so that later, at the bar, you can order without worrying that she'll give you the check when it comes."

After the bar is when the real work starts. "All the warm-up, I do on autopilot. No problem. What still takes work is the sex." According to Ernesto, women visit to Cuba for the Caribbean heat, and they're merciless about it. Sex at night, in the morning, before lunch, after lunch, in the shower, in the kitchen, on the ground, against a tree, in a bush, on the stairs. "You've got to drive them nuts, man. Six, seven, eight times a day. Only a Cuban can do that.

"How? Using my mind. I concentrate, man. I focus. I'm professional. It's sex, yeah, but I don't care about her tits, none of that. I'm asking myself, 'What's she going to remember later?' Every single thing I have in this world, I owe to my dick, man. That's the truth."

Ernesto trained for his role, in a way his roster of women couldn't possibly imagine. "You're not ready till you've fucked a chicken, man, a pig, a goat. Animals have hotter pussies than women. Any farm kid in the east knows that. If you want to learn to control yourself, to not come fast, you go make a chicken scream."

I ask, "Do you know how many foreign women you've had sex with?"

"No, man. I wish. My buddy asked the same question, and I couldn't even guess. I should've counted. But I can tell you it's a high number, since I'm not picky. She's just got to be foreign.

Fat or ugly isn't a problem. It's good, really, since those girls need it more."

* * *

The following summer, Ernesto spent a week at home in Baracoa. He didn't bring anybody with him. His mother says he only went out during the day to use the free internet downtown. Otherwise, he just sat by the living-room window, thinking about his father, spinning his new gold ring.

"He said he'd come to say goodbye," she says. "He told me he'd married a French woman, and he was leaving the country. He'd brought her to meet me the year before, but I really don't remember which one of the French girls it was."

HAVANA ISN'T FOR EVERYONE

All night long, Gretchen had a bad feeling. Her husband hadn't come home. Something must have happened. When the phone rang, she knew she was right.

She gripped the chair hard with her free hand. "Hey," her brother-in-law said over the phone, "Junior got arrested yesterday afternoon. But he didn't do anything wrong, I swear. We were eating lunch on Alfredo's porch and the cops came by, asked for our IDs, saw he was from Santiago, and took him away."

Junior Medina, thirty-four years old, spent that night in Vivac de Calabazar, a prison outside of Havana.

* * *

On Tuesday morning, Gretchen, who's twenty-nine, leaves her house in Diezmero, on the southeastern edge of Havana, with her daughters, who are eleven and seven, and her six-week-old son, her only child with Junior. They ride the bus to her mother's house in Cerro, in the center of the city. There, Gretchen drops off the kids, then goes to meet her brother-in-law to go to Vivac. The prison is in Bejucal, a suburb of Havana. To get there, you take a narrow, congested road filled with automobiles and men in horse-drawn wagons who are bringing relatives of the detainees to the prison for a fee. Cars shiver by the wagons, kicking up yellow dust from the rocky, pitted street.

I found Gretchen collapsed in the shade of the only tree growing near the prison. She was with Junior's brother and a woman whose son had been arrested for carrying a machete in public. They were all waiting until 2:00 p.m., when visiting hours start. Gretchen had already learned that her husband had neither temporary nor transitory residency in Havana, and so, having spent seventy-two hours in the capital of his country and lacking the legal right to more, he would be deported to the city of his birth.

* * *

Cuba's Decree 217, which became law in 1997, says that:

> Any individual born outside Havana who permanently inhabits that city without having been granted legal residency will be fined 300 pesos.
>
> Any individual born outside Havana who permanently inhabits that city without making him-or herself known to the civil registry office will be fined 200 pesos.
>
> Any owner of a dwelling inhabited by an individual born outside Havana who lives in the city without registration or legal residency will be fined 500 pesos. If the dwelling is in the municipalities of Old Havana, Central Havana, Cerro, or 10 de Octubre, the owner will be fined 1000 pesos.
>
> Any migrant discovered by authorities will be obligated to return to their legal home.

* * *

At noon, a rented Hyundai does a U-turn and parks at the

front gate of the prison. Four men get out of the car and argue with the guard to be allowed to give food to a family member imprisoned for attempting to illegally leave the country by sea. After having their request denied, they get back in the car and drive off, dust and frustration rising in their wake.

Next a woman comes and successfully drops off a box of cigarettes and a clean shirt for her husband, who's about to be deported for selling broomsticks on the street without a license. After her are a pair of women with a small boy. The guard, who seems to recognize them, looks for a name on a list, then asks them to wait. He jokes with them until two men with eastern accents approach the prison's barred windows to talk to the women and the child.

The guard has no gun, no baton, no pepper spray, no handcuffs. He wears a tight shirt and baggy pants. Although the sun is ferocious, he hardly wears his hat. When he's not searching for names on the roster of prisoners, he leans on the white gate and plays games on a cell phone in a pink case.

"All the easterners come here before getting deported," he tells me in an eastern accent. "You come to Havana illegally, you end up here. On Fridays, we send two buses east, with forty-five prisoners each, and we also send a train to Santiago at the start and end of the month.

"It's a hotel in there. It's better than those guys' houses. We've got a lot of cells and they're not big, but they have foam mattresses, plasma TVs, and as much water as they can drink, and they get a ten-minute visit once a week."

* * *

Havana's railway police chief runs his department from a station by the La Coubre terminal. His job is keeping the peace on the trains transporting detainees to the provinces where they were born. "By the time these individuals reach us, their misdemeanors have been investigated," he tells me. "Havana's neighborhoods are very highly patrolled. We don't see suspects until it's time for them to be deported, and we don't know what they're being deported for. We just deliver them to their destination. We ask them to remain in one car, but we don't handcuff them, and no one is mistreated along the way."

* * *

At 2:00, the guard lets the waiting relatives into the prison for their ten fleeting minutes. He leads them to the visiting room to wait for the detainees, who arrive shackled in pairs, Siamese twins linked by handcuffs and loose, dangling chains. As they approach, no one speaks: the only sounds are the squeaking cuffs and the rhythmic steps of men walking in unison; if one stumbles and pulls a chain, his partner will end up on the floor.

As soon as the guard unlocks the cuffs, the clock starts ticking. Junior asks about the baby before even giving Gretchen a kiss. As Gretchen talks, his eyes grow wet. His arrest isn't the only awful thing that's happened during their four years of marriage. Not long ago, they lost a one-year-old son. He was playing in the living room and grabbed the exposed electrical cord of a fan. It shorted, electrocuting the little boy.

Ten minutes isn't long enough for Junior to drink his coffee, let alone eat the rice and beans with pork that Gretchen and his brother brought him. He's got a guard hovering beside him the whole time. Before he is taken away, he tells his wife, "when I get to Santiago, I have to pay 3000 pesos for selling vegetables in Havana without a license."

* * *

Havana has struggled with overpopulation for several decades. Over the past thirty years, the population has doubled from one million inhabitants to over two million. The city is much more developed than any other part of the country, which draws people from the rural areas. According to government data, 41 percent of Cuba's internal migrants—some half a million people—live in Havana; 57 percent of them come from the east. Many end up in shantytowns.

* * *

Every Friday, Vivac's gates open at 9:00 a.m. to admit the buses that will take the latest batch of detainees away. Inside the prison, a guard reads names from a list, telling the inmates when to board. It happens in reverse geographical order: the sooner your name gets called, the longer your journey will last.

Junior Medina gets on the bus early, lucking into a window seat for his 765-kilometer ride. He's sitting on the left side of the bus, surrounded by other Santiaguinos. All morning, he'll be in the sun; all afternoon, the shade.

Junior's seatmate, Pacho, is thirty-six, Black, with dreadlocks and gold teeth. He wears a knit Rasta cap that he never takes off: not at Vivac, not on the bus, and not at his home in Camino, a neighborhood in Santiago. His house there leans like the Tower of Pisa.

Pacho is wearing slides and one sock. Several months ago, he tripped on a rock and cut his toe, which got infected and had to be amputated. "In Havana," he shares, "I sold hammock rope and chairs on Calle Monte. I bought them under the table at a factory and marked them up 100 percent. I never had a room in the city, so I'd go to a building with a garage and pay the guard ten pesos to let me sleep in a car until 4:00 a.m."

Pacho's already been deported once before. When he got kicked out of Havana the first time, he arrived in Santiago at 2:00 a.m., went home, gave his mother a kiss, and by 5:00 that same morning was on a bus back to Havana. He tells me that he isn't going to fight his way back this time, as his health isn't strong enough anymore.

Behind Junior is Piquirí, a wiry thirty-three-year-old whose dark skin is covered in low-quality tattoos. He has a marijuana leaf on his shoulder, an illegible English word on his stomach, more text on his arms, neck and thighs. He's Pacho's neighbor in Santiago, and he, too, sold hammock chairs in Havana. "Castro and his brother are criminals," he says. "Calling us illegal in our own country, banning us from our capital—you know what that's like? You're scared all the time. You're running from the cops, who all have hard-ons for picking up easterners even though they're from the east, too.

"I got arrested by the Capitol. A paddy wagon pulled up and the cops grabbed anyone they could, shoved us in, and took anyone who didn't have a Havana ID to jail."

Before he was deported, Piquirí had started dating a girl from Havana, but he assumes his legal status is going to end the relationship. "I'm just going to keep getting deported unless we get married, and we only got together a month ago. She's not going to invite me to come live in her house now."

Sitting alone in the rear left-hand corner of the bus is Luis Sarmiento. He's fifty-five, with topographic wrinkles covering his amber skin. He's almost too drunk to talk, and when he does try to speak, he's incomprehensible. In Santiago, his neighbors call him Luis the Drunk. He's spent more than twenty years shuttling across the island to earn a living.

"I'm not a criminal," he tells me later, after the bus ride. "I was selling food in Havana, but that's done now. Deported again. I can't remember how many times this has happened."

He's drinking rum on the sidewalk with his friends. He'd said he would let me interview him in his house, but now, without warning, he cuts our conversation short. "I already did prison time over this," he declares, "and I'm not getting sent back because of you."

* * *

At the front of the left side of the bus is Glenda, twenty-six, a tall, oval-faced Black woman with braids down to her waist. It's her second deportation. She says the judge gave her a warning this time: if she gets detained again, she'll go to jail for four years. (Junior tells me later that Glenda didn't say a word during the entire bus ride. She just stared out the window, as if searching for something or someone.)

Glenda was arrested for prostitution. She was roaming the city's main streets at night, signaling to drivers, waiting until one rolled down his window to negotiate. She works alone, but the last time she went to Havana, it was different. "I was young," she says, "and I took my friend's advice. She's in jail now. I was in the capital, no job, and this was what I had to do. But it was hard. I was at Monte and Cienfuegos, not earning shit. My boyfriend kept all the money I made."

Her "boyfriend" was really her pimp. He ran eleven women, all migrants, out of a house-turned-motel at the corner of Calle Monte and Cienfuegos. Some days, no customers came; if that happened, or if the men who did come chose other girls, Glenda didn't have enough to afford a meal. Other days, however, she could have sex with four men in three hours.

At the intersection of Calle Monte and Cienfuegos, pimps roam the sidewalks, mumbling about their girls' availability, or sit outside house-motels and let their underlings bring the johns to them. When a client arrives, the pimp leads him down a hallway lined with doors or curtains to a waiting group of girls. On seeing the john, the women leap to attention as if they were soldiers and he was a general. With their eyes fixed on the client, they touch their mouths, wave him closer, spin to show him their curves, try to seduce him with clichés. Once he chooses a prostitute, the john pays her "boyfriend" $5.00, only $2.00 of which goes to the girl.

Glenda's twin sister still lives with their mother, a nurse in Santiago. Glenda, when she's not in Havana, lives with her nineteen-month-old daughter.

* * *

Junior sits behind Ever, an agitated, brown-skinned thirty-four-year-old with a cut on his face. He talks endlessly about how cursed his life is, how he's always honest, how he never hides anything. To prove this, he announces that he's a hustler as proudly if he'd gotten a PhD in the subject.

Ever is from Santa Elena, a poor community in Santiago. Children play barefoot on its unpaved streets, and you can smoke a joint in broad daylight, but can't get a jug of drinkable water. Ever and his mother have been homeless since a palm tree crushed their house during Hurricane Sandy. The government never offered them shelter or reimbursement, so they moved into an abandoned carpentry shop that has no bathroom and only half a roof—which is to say that they essentially live outdoors.

"Cuban salaries won't get you a pair of flip-flops," he tells me. "All you can do is scrape by. I was going to beaches like

Santa Lucía, Pesquero, Varadero. I thought I'd try Havana, but I just got kicked out." The reason Ever went to Havana in the first place was to buy goods with the money he earned in Varadero. His plan was to sell the stuff in Santiago. "In Varadero, I'd get to the beach by 9:30 a.m. and just walk. I never carried anything, but I let the tourists know that I could get whatever they wanted: a cigar, a woman, didn't matter. What was hard was that when the tourists asked for something, I had to get it on the beach, and there were always cops around.

"I slept on the beach in Varadero, on a cardboard box," he continues. "I'd pay the hotel employees a dollar to bring me buffet leftovers or ask tourists to give me a sandwich." During tourist season, the cops guard the beach night and day, so Ever would go to a building downtown, tell the night watchman his story, give the guy some cash and his ID as collateral, and sleep on the top floor until dawn

Ever tells me that he wore shredded, ratty shorts, an old shirt and holey sandals when he was working. His wardrobe projected his poverty, inspiring tourists "to give me some clothes since I live so badly. I always say I've got two kids, too, and a sick mom."

Ever has a nephew, but no children. And although his mother lives out in the elements, she's in good health.

* * *

In Cerro, the municipality in Havana where Gretchen's family lives, Santería drummers gather to perform *toque de santo*, a ceremony of drumming and dancing that celebrates the orichas of the Cuban Lucumi tradition. Colorfully dressed worshippers drink beer and rum, spilling from the house where the ritual is happening onto the sidewalk and into the street. A little boy dances, and dogs wrestle on the corner.

At 8:00 a.m., the electricity went out, and now, at nightfall, it still hasn't returned. On the roof of Gretchen's parents' stucco home, which is swelteringly hot, her father tries to rock his six-week-old grandson to sleep. Inside, Gretchen, her mother Bárbara, her brother-in-law, and some friends celebrate the news: Junior called from Santiago. His brother there paid his fine, and he's free.

Bárbara is a medium, and that night she dreams of the dead talking about the subjects that are associated with the numbers in *Charada Cubana*. When she wakes up, she plays two numbers and hits the jackpot. One of her numbers is forty-one.

It means prison.

THE PHARMACY ODYSSEY

Ramiro is already awake when the alarm rings at 3:45 a.m. He gets out of bed, goes to the kitchen, and brews himself some coffee. He lights a cigarette and looks through the wooden blinds at a flickering electric streetlight Today is Tuesday, and Ramiro, who's seventy, is up this early so that he can get in line at the state pharmacy in his neighborhood and—if he's there in time—bring home the medicines his family needs. He began this ritual—if you can call something where you have no choice a ritual—in 2016, when the Cuban health system's ability to supply pharmaceuticals to the population went into a precipitous decline.

After his coffee and cigarette, Ramiro showers, gets dressed, and kisses his wife, who's fast asleep and bundled in a sheet, on the forehead. She's seventy-seven, and has heart disease. Closing the door, he slips into the other bedroom, where his forty-two-year-old son, who was diagnosed with HIV twenty years ago, is sleeping.

* * *

Ramiro leaves before sunrise, walking the six dark blocks to Calle 16 in Vedado. On the way, he lights another cigarette and plays a game of spotting the gleaming eyes of cats hiding under cars.

By the time he gets to the pharmacy at five past four, fourteen people are already in line. It's not technically a line yet, since the doors won't open until eight o'clock. Whenever a new person arrives, they ask who came most recently, take note of their own position, and sit down to wait for the hours to pass.

Slowly, the group turns into a crowd. Seniors sit on rags or broken-down cardboard boxes, their wrinkled faces tired and pained. Adolescents and young adults mill around. They are all soon joined by a woman who shows up just after Ramiro. She's carrying her sleeping son, who's seven years old, and she's visibly exhausted. Somebody gets her a cardboard box to place her son on. Her name is Alba, and she's thirty-four years old.

When Alba sets the boy down, he rouses and blinks at his surroundings, surely baffled by where he is and why so many strangers are looking at him sympathetically. But tiredness beats curiosity, and he closes his eyes again. Alba settles herself beside him, creating a disconcerting image: a child sleeping on a piece of trash in his school uniform—red shorts, white shirt, blue bandana—as his mother strokes his hair.

Alba is divorced. She and her son are both asthmatics. When their medications run out, she has to get up early and take him to the pharmacy with her; he'd be terrified if he woke up and she was not there. In a few hours, she tells me, she can take her son to school; she'll have a much less stressful time waiting in line when she doesn't have to keep an eye on him.

Ramiro, overhearing our conversation, tosses a half-smoked cigarette to the ground and grinds it out with his foot.

* * *

After the Revolution, Fidel Castro created a system of clinics and pharmacies, as well as international medical brigades that went to poorer nations that were dealing with natural disasters. Cuban medicine was among the government's proudest achievement.

But during the Special Period, Cuba's health system, like all its other institutions, started to deteriorate, and it's only gotten worse since then. While Cubans can still go to the doctor without paying, get decent treatment and take their ration card to the state pharmacy once a month, signs of decay are readily apparent. For example, several months before I went to the pharmacy with Ramiro, the government decided that after any medical consultation or procedure, patients were required to take home a document outlining the price of the care they'd received. People got upset, as everyone thought that this was the beginning of the end of universal public health (though the government quickly clarified that it was just a campaign by the Ministry of Public Health to raise awareness of the nation's spending on medical treatment.)

The crisis in Cuban medicine began after the country started receiving dramatically less oil from Venezuela, which in turn affected the island's drug manufacturers. María Cristina Lara Bastanzuri, the National Director of Technology and Medicines at the Ministry of Public Health, said in an interview that the oil shortage's "effects on industry have direct repercussions for the pharmacy network," meaning that many factories have closed their doors. Bastanzuri added that "the industry is also suffering from the U.S. blockade, which raises prices, since rather than trading in dollars, drug manufacturers have to buy materials from very far away, get them sent by plane, and wait a long time for them to arrive. All of this drives up costs, which the government then has to absorb."

Cuba's drug manufacturers produce 53 percent of the 801 medicines that should be in a pharmacy's base stock. All the rest, the government imports. Forty-seven percent of the manufacturers' products are set aside for the state pharmacy network. Rita María García Almaguer, operations director at the state-run research group BioCubaFarma, told *Granma* (the official newspaper of the Central Committee of the Communist Party) that "the industry's unreliability in producing pharmaceuticals is the result of improper financing structures, which make it difficult to negotiate for raw materials, packaging, and other supplies."

* * *

Since the start of the medicine crisis, the country's 2148 pharmacies have set aside one day a week to sell the drugs the Ministry of Public Health provides. The pharmacy that Ramiro uses does it on Tuesdays, which means its customers start getting agitated on Mondays, as no one knows what medicines the state will deliver that week. The only option is to wait hours in line, without any guarantee of getting what you need.

"You have to come," says Ofelia, the person at the front of the line. "No matter what's going on, you have to come, because there's not enough medicine to go around." She arrived fourteen hours before the pharmacy opens. She's Black, fifty-nine years old and retired. "My husband's traveling," she explains, "but usually we switch off. I come on Monday night to get in line. He relieves me and sleeps here, and then after the sun's up I take over so that he can go to work."

Ofelia has a shawl to protect herself from the morning chill, a sheet to sit on, and her son's old army backpack, which holds a thermos of coffee, two empty containers that held her dinner and breakfast, a bottle of boiled drinking water and a bottle of tap water for rinsing her Tupperware and washing her face after waking. "I'd love to be asleep at home right now," she says, "but that's irrelevant. I have to be here."

* * *

Magalys, twenty-nine, has worked at the pharmacy for a year. She started around the time the medicine crisis began, and through one of the building's windows, tells me, "It was worse then. Now we get more medications, but Cubans are hypochondriacs. We self-medicate and we hoard pills. Dipyrone, especially. In a Cuban house, dipyrone is queen."

According to the Ministry of Public Health, the drug industry would have to manufacture between 84 and 86 million tablets of dipyrone, a powerful painkiller and fever-reducer, to satisfy the monthly demand. "Our plants sometimes struggle with that quantity," García Almaguer told *Granma*, "and there were certain issues with debt, but we're increasing production and expect to deliver the necessary amount of dipyrone shortly."

Magalys wears a tight white uniform and a nurse's cap. She snaps gum as she says defensively, "It isn't our fault. Pharmacies are the end of the chain. We just sell what the government gives us."

She and her colleagues alternate two days of work with two days of rest, plus a twenty-four-hour guard shift once a week. Magalys is on guard right now. She's got bags under her eyes, and her hair has begun to escape her cap. "I hate having guard duty on Mondays," she says. "I hate watching this scene. So many people scrambling for pills. I really hope the situation keeps improving."

"What do your bosses say?" I ask.

"That it's already better, and it's going to get better still."

"So it was worse before?"

"Before," she says, "we had nothing on the shelves but cough syrup and condoms."

* * *

At 8:00, one of Magalys's colleagues unlocks the pharmacy, and the street erupts. Nearly all the 100 or so people waiting leap to their feet like soldiers called to battle, and what was an orderly line is now a shoving mob. "Control yourselves!" somebody says, and an employee shouts, "If you don't calm down, nobody gets anything."

Once the crowd settles, a pharmacy worker starts passing out tickets to organize the line, which wraps around the corner. A man who is waiting tells me, "Sometimes you can get a ticket and still not have a chance to buy the drug you need. I've gone two months without my blood-pressure medication."

Beside the pharmacy are a line of pay phones linked by an iron pole on which new arrivals sit. One woman says to her neighbor, "It'll just be luck if we get anything. Would you ever have thought that in Cuba, you'd have to get up at dawn to not die?"

"I can't understand it," her neighbor replies. "All the medicines are available on the black market, but you can't get them at the pharmacy. How could that be?"

A national audit done by the Ministry of Public Health yields the answer: prescription forgeries, illegal medication sales and other forms of corruption at the state pharmacies.

* * *

Ramiro is nearly at the front of the line. We can't speak over the commotion, but he keeps giving me conspiratorial looks. I step away from the line, and he joins me to light a cigarette. As he smokes, he grips my arm and says very quietly, "If my pension were bigger, I'd buy drugs somewhere else, but I can't, and my wife’s heart is shot. She’d die on me if I didn’t come here. As it is, we never get all the pills she needs. We do get my son’s HIV medication, though. He’s a national priority. I’m telling you, the government takes care of people with HIV.” García Almaguer said in *Granma* that “[w[e’re dedicated to pharmaceutical coverage for gravely ill Cubans, such as cancer patients, and those living with HIV. We’ve maintained stable delivery of medications for them for some time.”

After Ramiro is done with his cigarette, I separate myself from the crowd and watch him enter the pharmacy. Seven minutes later, he comes out. He scans the street but doesn’t spot me until I wave him over. He tells me that two of the drugs his wife needs were already gone. His expression is that of a man staring into the abyss. Not until a bus goes by does he seem to return.

“I hate what’s going on in Cuba,” he says. “But I can’t quit fighting for my wife.”

THE UNBREAKABLE ARGELIA FELLOVE

Alberto is half-dressed, his belt unbuckled, his shirt off. He is wearing red lipstick, but the rest of his face is not yet made up. He left his hand mirror at home, so he's going to have to finish getting ready in the women's room, since América is hogging the only mirror in the men's room. At Club Tikoa, a subterranean bar on Vedado's Calle 23, there's no backstage, so the performers have to get into costume in the bathroom.

While he waits in line for the ladies' room, Alberto does what he can without being able to see his reflection. He gets out his makeup kit and, standing in the dark, unventilated hallway, puts on foundation, buckles a watch's leather strap around his right wrist and hangs a fake gold chain around his neck. Sweat drips down his face, the heat made worse by the binder he is wearing. "I washed it too late yesterday," he says irritably, "and it's still damp."

When the bathroom finally becomes free, Alberto bolts inside and shuts the door. It's a shadowy room with the revoltingly strong smell of urine. On the wall hangs a wide mirror with a freshly painted wood frame. Alberto regards himself as he silently outlines and draws in his eyebrows, adds to the foundation he put on in the hallway and wrestles his hair into a small bun. These layers of makeup are like scar tissue, healing the wounds of the past.

Alberto's hair is cut into an undercut. This is for practical reasons: when he shaves the lower half of his head, he keeps the hairs, which he then attaches to his chin with wig glue. He lines the fake beard up with a knife, though once, he says, "I dropped the knife down the drain and had to use my ID."

* * *

While Alberto and América prepare, the audience trickles in. At 3:00, the "Big Saturday" show will begin. It's a refuge from the outside world for the attendees, even though Club Tikoa is a dark, gloomy dump. Behind the bar is a young Black woman with no color in her outfit or her cheeks. The only drink she serves is warm rum, as there is no ice.

It costs ten pesos to see the show, which runs until 7:00 p.m. Outside, the August sun is devastatingly hot, but inside, a dripping, grumbling air conditioner has the crowd shivering in their seats. Fluorescent lights blur the assembled faces, but not enough to conceal the fact that everyone here appears to be at least fifty years old.

* * *

Alberto is ready. He's wearing an outfit straight out of the 1940s: white shirt and hat, pinstriped beige jacket, a caramel-colored belt that matches his pointed shoes. América, who's in his sixties, is still in his underwear and stockings, having joined Alberto in the ladies' room. "We've got the world spinning backwards," he jokes to Alberto, lifting an eyebrow in the mirror. "Men in women's clothes, women in men's. Right, Argelia?"

* * *

Argelia Fellove Hernández has no idea how she made it to the age of fifty-two.

Twenty years ago, she was depressed and miserable. It was

2005, Fidel Castro was still in power, and Cuban society was corrosively homophobic. But after Raúl Castro took control of the country in 2008, his daughter Mariela was put in charge of the National Center for Sexual Education, or CENESEX, an institution that, since its founding in 1989, has fought for LGBTQ+ rights.

Around that time, a friend of Argelia's suggested she join a circle of gay and bisexual women, nearly all intellectuals, who met at CENESEX. The group was called Oremi, which means "friend" in Yoruba. In addition to offering emotional support, the group also put together courses, workshops and conferences to help its members face the judgmental attitudes of society with dignity. "It only took one meeting to understand that all these women shared my struggle, "Argelia recalls. "Right away, I got stronger and started fighting my own prejudices."

Argelia became a regular at Oremi. On top of bolstering her spirit, the group also made her want to address her past. "I had to break my silence," she says, "to empower myself." She became a LGBTQ+ leader, eventually becoming coordinator of the Havana chapter of the Network for Bisexual and Lesbian Women (NFBALW). She rattles off the organization's goals like a set of commandments: "Promoting queer visibility; providing sex education and preventing sexually transmitted diseases and HIV; giving girls like us tools and resources; protecting our rights as a minority; and opposing gender-based violence."

Every province in Cuba has a NFBALW chapter. The one in Havana meets monthly so that the members can support each other. Argelia refers to their conversations as "stone soup," after the tale of a town whose members all contribute an ingredient to a collective pot.

* * *

While joining Oremi transformed Argelia's life, it was still an institutional project controlled by the government. She knew that she wanted something of her own.

The Oremi meetings and conferences were often tense events. To add some levity, Argelia began performing at them in drag. Her repertoire consisted of four ballads that were big at the time: Alezandre Pires's "Es Por Amor;" Alejandro Sanz's "Amiga Mía;" Alejandro Fernández's "Me Dediqué a Perderte;" and DLG's "A Puro Dolor."

She performed in clothes that she borrowed from one of her brothers-in-law. He resisted loaning them to her at first—he was a member of Sociedad Secreta Abakuá, an all-male secret religious sect—but eventually gave in.

Argelia's was so charismatic that the audiences quickly forgot that she was a woman. Soon her alter ego had acquired a name: Alberto.

But Alberto didn't last long. "Discrimination and exclusion were givens back then," Argelia explains. "Drag was almost unheard of. I wouldn't have had enough spaces to perform in if I'd tried to take it seriously, so I told myself it wasn't worth my time."

* * *

Over the next decade, Cuban society started shifting, and the government began to sanction aboveground gathering places for queer people. In this new climate, CENESEX greenlit a dream of Argelia's: a school for drag kings.

The school met—and still meets—once a month at Havana's Acapulco Theater. From the moment it began, Alberto was back. "My whole body wanted it," Argelia says. "I had to start performing again." But Alberto wasn't alone; with seven companions, he created a laboratory for drag kings, launching a movement in Cuba.

Alberto wanted nothing more than to make people dance. While he still performed a few romantic ballads, his songs became calculated to get everyone up, moving and connecting. His calling cards were rumba and Cuban salsa—so much so that his audience started calling him Alberto el Salsero, though Argelia adds some messaging to the name by spelling it Sal-*zero*: zero discrimination, zero violence, zero segregation.

* * *

CENESEX holds its annual Pride Day on May 11th. The day usually ends with a conga line against homophobia, but on the twelve annual celebration in 2019, the government called the conga line off. When protestors demanded the right to dance, the police reacted with a brutal crackdown. By the end of the demonstration, there were bloody faces, cops choking civilians and gay Cubans getting dragged to jail by teams of policemen. "We only get one day a year," Argelia says. "If we had more, maybe we wouldn't all have protested, but as it is, the whole network came out. It was a nonviolent demonstration. All the brutality only happened because the cops had already decided it should.

"We might not have UMAPs anymore," Argelia adds, "but our society is still homophobic, patriarchal, macho, heterosexist, misogynistic and racist." She's talking about the forced labor camps that the government ran from 1965 to 1968 in the province of Camagüey, interning and "reeducating" gay people, prostitutes, pimps, delinquents, religious believers and dissidents. Although there's exact count on the number of Cubans who were sent to these camps, the majority of studies suggest around 25,000.

Raúl Castro, then the head of Cuba's Army, said in an April 1966 speech that, "[o]ur Military Units to Aid Production [UMAPs] contained a number of young people who had conducted themselves poorly in life, who had been led down an antisocial path by bad influences at home or in the media. By including them, we helped them return to a course of full integration in society."

* * *

Despite launching her drag school, Argelia still desired to develop a project independent of Oremi. She wanted it to be inclusive, itinerant and able to grow. That was when she came up with Afrodiverso, which, Argelia explains, is "aimed at empowering Black and mixed-race lesbians by allowing them to explore their history, their African origins and their essence as women through drag."

The 2012 census found that Cuba's 11.2 million inhabitants were 64.1 percent white, 26.6 percent mixed race and 9.3 percent Black. However, not even the census-takers considered these results trustworthy, as all the data was self-reported, and many Cubans refuse to recognize their African heritage. A 2018 study by the National Center of Genetic Medicine concluded that all Cubans, regardless of appearance, are of mixed-race descent, and that the population's overall origins are 2 percent Chinese, 8 percent indigenous, 20 percent African (mainly from Benin, Nigeria, Cameroon, Gabon and Angola) and 70 percent European (mainly from Spain and certain parts of Italy).

While the aim of Afrodiverso is to combat racial discrimination against and among Cuba's queer women, Argelia also uses the organization to improve the lives of vulnerable citizens, including drag performance whenever she can. For instance, through Afrodiverso, she founded a children's dance group in Barrio Azul, a dilapidated suburb of Havana. She also spends Children's Day in Melena del Sur in Mayabeque Province, leading kids' storytelling workshops that end in a big party with gifts for the attendees.

For all this work, Argelia receives not one peso. "My payment is spiritual," she says. She funds Afrodiverso herself, aided only by friends who donate materials ranging from colored pencils, crayons, toys, cloth and snacks to used clothes and shoes that Argelia sells to purchase the rest of what she needs.

* * *

Argelia's grandmother, Matilde Hernández, worked as a maid in the home of the Arrechea's, one of the wealthiest families in Sancti Spíritus Province. José Arrechea, the family patriarch, developed an interest in Matilde, who was beautiful and ill-equipped to resist him. He'd drag her to some hut or field on his property, and demand sex. One of those forced encounters led to a pregnancy, and so Argelia's mother, Trinidad Margarita Hernández, was born.

Trinidad grew up in the kitchen, patio and servants' quarters of the Arrechea plantation. José never admitted that he was her father, though he occasionally let her play with her white sisters upstairs.

Argelia got the last name Fellove from her father, who came from a Congolese family that emigrated to Cuba via France. He brought Trinidad to Havana, where they had eight children: three girls and five boys. Argelia was born in 1967, though her mother didn't register her with the government until her husband died of a heart attack in 1970.

Argelia's father was a welder. When he passed, all he left behind was his pension: 180 pesos a month. By then Trinidad had medical issues and couldn't work, which meant that she had no other income to support her eight children, or to get them out of La Construcción, a "hot" neighborhood of gambling, drinking, brawling, robberies and partying located in in Boyeros, a municipality in the south of Havana.

Argelia's childhood was very dark. As she speaks to me about it, her face contracts and her tone grows as sharp as a whip. "At home, my mom hit, hit, hit, hit, hit," she says. Raising eight children in a tiny shack and living in destitution was just too much for Trinidad. She often lost control of herself. If the children annoyed her—if one was loud, or hungry, or inquisitive—she'd get an electrical cord, line up all eight kids on their hands and knees, and beat their bottoms until she heard sobs. She'd also pinch the girls' breasts.

Unsurprisingly, the children reacted by becoming so aggressive that the house became a battlefield: pots and pans flying, stones as weapons, sticks and bats everywhere. Trinidad would watch calmly, doing her nails in a chair while one of her kids hit another with a mallet. "One of my brothers is schizophrenic," Argelia tells me, "and is addicted to getting hit. When he was bored, he'd go spit at a cop, get the shit kicked out of him, and come home from jail the next day in a great mood."

Argelia attended primary school wearing an un-ironed, dirty uniform. She and one of her brothers took turns wearing a pair of men's boots. On the days when it wasn't her turn, Argelia wore broken flip-flops held together by a jump-rope cord. Her grades were never strong, since she couldn't study at home and was also abused by the other kids. "I got bullied at school and on the street," she recalls. "I got hit all the time, and once, a whole group of boys dragged me behind the school building and groped me over my clothes." The classroom was violent, too, as her teachers, natives of La Construcción, had likely grown up in situations not dissimilar to Argelia's, which is no excuse for disciplining children by hitting them with metal rulers or forcing them to kneel on peas or bottle caps in the corner of the room.

* * *

Every member of the Fellove family was anemic, as a 180-peso pension couldn't come close to putting eight meals on the table every day. A kind neighbor sometimes gave the family food; Argelia would drop by her house with a metal canteen, but she often had to bring it back empty. "I didn't go upstairs," she confesses. "Her son would wait in the stairwell and start jerking off if he saw me, so when he was around, I just left."

But none of those traumas affected her as much as what happened with her brother. Each night, she and her siblings slept on a straw mattress crawling with fleas and bugs, crammed together in a criss-cross arrangement that still couldn't fit all eight of them. One unlucky child always had to sleep alone, "and that's who my brother took to the bathroom to hurt," Argelia says.

Dámaso, the oldest child, was six feet tall by the time he was fourteen. Very early in the morning, he'd wake two of his siblings, including the one who was sleeping alone, and herd them into the bathroom, where he had a chair and a rope. What he did next was horrific. He'd make one brother or sister—he didn't discriminate—stand on the chair, then put the rope around their neck like a noose and give its loose end to the other sibling. He then penetrated the child on the chair, at the same time ordering the child with the rope to pull on the end if their sibling made a sound. After he was done with the first child, he made them switch places. "We had to suck his dick. We had to swallow. Not just semen," Argelia adds. "Urine, too." She's crying now. Her voice cracks. Her body shakes.

While Dámaso raped his siblings, their mother slept soundly in the next room. She was aware of what she was sleeping through, but pretended it wasn't happening. Dámaso threatened her constantly, and she was afraid that he would kill her if she intervened, and so she let him turn her other children's nights into a living hell. "I got gastroenteritis once and went to the hospital," Argelia says, after having paused to get some air. "I nearly died." Her little body—she was four when the abuse started—couldn't bear such extreme violence.

It wasn't only the children that Dámaso abused. Once, when Argelia and her younger brothers were playing hide and seek, she ran into her grandmother's room and encountered another scene that she can't ever erase: Matilde facedown and naked, half-conscious, Dámaso raping her on sheets stained with feces.

Only Gertrudis, Argelia's oldest sister, confronted Dámaso and their mother, "but our mom just smacked her," Argelia said. "After that, we knew we had no hope." Gertrudis managed to leave home for high school, "and my other sister, Griselda, had to be Dámaso's girlfriend to get him to leave us alone."

Dating his sister made Dámaso abuse his other siblings less often, but it didn't stop him completely. "Once he tried to grab me in the living room and I ran. He chased me, throwing alcohol and matches. I still escaped, though," Argelia says. She had to be hospitalized for the burns she received.

* * *

Argelia was able to leave home to attend secondary school. Going to boarding school provided her with independence, separation from her family's chaos, and, no less importantly, a full meal every day. Her dream was to eventually study physical education in college (she had already missed an opportunity to become an athlete when she was younger: she had been recruited to a sports school because of her height—as an adult, she's five foot ten—but her mother never signed the necessary forms). However, her grades weren't good enough, so she had to settle for going to technical school. There, she learned health statistics by studying the rates and determinants of infant mortality, live birth and illness.

After school, she worked at various clinics until one day in 1988, when a man stopped her on the street. He told her he was signing up young women for a course in refereeing and asked if she was interested. It was like a divine intervention. Finally, her dream of a life in sports might come true.

Argelia started refereeing at a national level, distinguishing herself so quickly that she was selected as one the judges for the 1991 Pan American Games and the 1992 IAAF World Cup in Athletics, both of which were held in Havana. (She still treasures a yellowed magazine clipping which shows her serving as the finish line judge for a gold medal race at the Pan American Games.)

Her supervisors, as a reward and for encouragement, gave Argelia a gift: they would help her attend college for physical education. She was elated, but unfortunately only made it through three years, due to continuing problems with her family. A few of her siblings—including Dámaso—were now in prison, while the rest were still at home, living with various boyfriends, girlfriends and children. Aggression and physical violence were prevalent at the house, and Argelia couldn't concentrate on her schoolwork because of what was happening. "My memory was useless," she says. "I had to drop out."

Argelia would often take food to some of her incarcerated siblings, which she only did because her mother begged her. Gertrudis scolded Argelia for giving in to Trinidad. On Argelia's thirty-third birthday, Gertrudis, after a few beers, told her sister, "You were too young to remember this, but when Dámaso went to jail when we were little, Mom brought us there so that he could do stuff to us." During these visits, she continued, their mother stood lookout, making sure the prison guards didn't interrupt her oldest son abusing her other children.

Once Gertrudis was done talking, Argelia asked her for a hug. "I'd never hugged her before. We never learned affection. We just knew how to hit."

* * *

Argelia came to hate men. Without meaning to, she had projected the trauma she'd lived through onto every man she saw. If a man honked at her while she was biking, she'd shout back, "asshole!" If she heard a child crying, she'd look in strangers' windows, unable to relax until she'd seen for herself that they were all right. If she saw a man walking alone with a child, she'd trail them until she decided he wasn't a threat, no matter how far she had to go. "I had a lot of trauma," she tells me. "I'm doing better now, but I still struggle with the knowledge that our legal system just lets predators go. If they behave in prison, they get out—no treatment, no social worker, nothing. A man who raped his child can go straight back home."

* * *

Argelia finally managed to fully separate herself from her family when she moved to Párraga, in Arroyo Naranjo, which is southwest of La Construcción. It's not far from Havana, but the area is rural, dominated by Afro-Cuban religion: Santería, Palo Monte and the Sociedad Secreta Abakuá.

In Párraga, Argelia lives in a shack that she restored herself, installing a kitchen counter, tiling the bathroom and putting in electricity—though a bottle so coated with candle wax that it looks like a snow drift still sits on top of the fridge. On the walls, are lanterns and pride flags. She decorated the front door with used CDs and painted an old iron red, which she displays on her windowsill.

While she lives in a new place, much of her surroundings are familiar. "It's just fighting, drinking, partying," she says of Párraga. "Sometimes I hear gunshots at night." Párraga, she has sadly learned, is virtually the same as La Construcción, except for one key difference: Párraga's dirt roads are overrun with wandering, dejected children, born into the void of marginality, with nowhere to go and nothing to do.

According to UNICEF's Children's Rights and Business Atlas, Arroyo Naranjo is home to over 12,000 minors, and ranks fourth lowest of all Cuban municipalities in children living with their parents (30.53 percent), and third highest for children living without parents (19.98 percent). For Argelia, these children are like versions of her past self, roaming the litter-strewn streets, dirty and uncared-for, avoiding the shouts and beatings that await them at home.

* * *

Half a block from Argelia's house is an abandoned park, which, like her home, she has also tried to restore. She hacked through the overgrown weeds with a machete and garlanded its one tree, a big flamboyant, with soda cans that she artfully cut to look like palm nuts, and tied together with cassette tape. She reinstalled the rusted fence that had been lying on the ground and gave it a new coat of paint. Somehow, she secured a streetlight. She whitewashed the flamboyant's trunk, dragged a giant rock to the entrance, and wrote AFRODIVERSO on its side. On a disused piece of metal, she engraved a variation on the lyrics of a song by Teresita Fernández, Cuba's most famous children's singer: *Vamos, amiguitxs, a cantar, porque tenemos el corazón feliz.* (Come on my friends, let's sing because our hearts are happy).

Argelia started teaching classes for the children of Párraga: papier-maché, ceramics, sewing, drawing, singing. On weekends, she lugs a speaker to the park and gets the kids to dance until dusk, when Alberto emerges for a culturally enriching drag show. "My project is really about the love, self-expression and the freedom I never had growing up," Argelia explains. "I needed options, and so do these children. Before Afrodiverso, none of them had any choices. A lot of didn't get any affection. I'd see them kicking rocks, digging in the trash, gambling, working on farms like grown men."

Afrodiverso has made such a positive impact that the Communist Party of Arroyo Naranjo has assisted Argelia in upgrading the park, providing garbage cans, benches, a swing, a jungle gym, a roundabout and a retired Party member to guard the park. Her name is Nancy Fuentes, and she's fifty-eight, with gray hair and a permanent sunburn. She and two of the park's other neighbors were the only ones to lend Argelia a hand when she began fixing it up. The rest went on drinking their rum, selling avocados door to door and cranking their reggaeton as loud as they could. "We'd be working," Nancy recalls, "and our neighbors would walk by without turning their heads."

However, this wasn't casual indifference—the residents of Párraga were actively shunning Argelia. Nancy, who was born and raised here, explains that her community initially rejected the very thought of a lesbian volunteering with children. "We're just not educated," Nancy tells me. "Or that's what the news always says. Me, I get along with everybody. I don't see what gives one person the right to tell another person how to live or what to do. Not even if it's your kid. A parent who rejects a gay child—that's not a real parent. You have to accept your children for who they are." She adds that, "I don't care who sees me helping Argelia, or kissing her hello, or going to her house."

* * *

Sun bounces from Argelia's scissor blade into her eyes. She bobs her head, annoyed. She's got a sewing workshop starting soon, and, as usual, she's setting up before the children arrive, sitting on a wooden bench surrounded by cloth, thread, paper, pencils and little shears. She's dressed comfortably in running shoes, shorts, a light jacket, a baseball cap with a pride flag, a fanny pack and a shirt that says SCHOOLS WITHOUT HOMOPHOBIA AND TRANSPHOBIA. Reggaeton plays softly from her portable speaker.

Her classroom is a corner of the park. She's covered the ground with cardboard boxes recycled from a bodega. Overhead hangs a roof made of stitched-together nylon sacks. At first, the classes she taught were filled with chaos. Instead of listening, the kids talked, fought, threw dirt, and caught lizards and put them in each other's clothes. "I had to teach them manners,"

Argelia recalls. "None of them knew to say 'Hello,' or 'Thank you,' or how to show respect, or work together, or share. If one brought some bread or water, it didn't occur to them to offer it to the rest."

But the children eventually learned, and Argelia became known to them as *Profe*—"teacher."

"Morning, *Profe*," says ten-year-old Lazarito, the first to arrive.

"Did you sleep okay, *Profe*?" asks Flavia, age eight.

"What are we doing today, *Profe*?" says Alejandrito, age five, and so it goes with Eddiel, three, and Luisito, Barbarito and Yankiel, all of whom are ten.

Once class is underway, I ask Luisito, "Do you like sewing?"

"No," he says dryly.

"So why are you here?"

"Bored."

"What do you like to do?"

Luisito is tired, though it's only mid-morning. He's on school break, and he got up at dawn. Argelia tells me that his uncle takes him to husk corn on a nearby farm that sells tamale.

"I like sewing. Drawing's better, though."

"Are you good at it?"

"My drawings are the best," he says proudly. "Ask *Profe*. She can show you the one of the woman sweeping her dirty house and the one of the trash collector on the corner."

Barbarito, who wears earrings, a camouflage cap, a bracelet and an imitation gold chain, holds up his cloth, on which Argelia has instructed the children to sew other, smaller pieces of cloth, and says, "*Profe*, what is this?"

"A tapestry," she answers. "You can put it on the fridge, or use it as a curtain in the bathroom, or put it on your bed so your feet don't get the sheets dirty."

Flavia, who's already done, wraps her tapestry around her head like a turban. "I like reggaeton," she informs me. "My grandmother wants to hear 'Guantanamera' on the radio, but I tell her, no, it's too old."

* * *

Following class, the male students gather by a dumpster a few blocks away to play marbles. They are surrounded by cow pies, construction debris, rotten food, dead rats and an omnipresent swarm of flies. "We're playing for keeps," Luisito tells me. "No messing around." He's clutching a five-peso bill he earned selling marbles, which are each worth twenty cents each. For keeps means you give one up if you lose.

After about half an hour, the boys are bored. One announces that he has to go: it's time to steal avocados to sell. I tell him I'm going to tell Argelia, and Lazarito, the group spokesman, shakes his head. "Okay, okay, okay, we'll go to school and play soccer. Don't mention the avocados to *Profe*. She'll get upset."

* * *

With one hand, Argelia wheels a suitcase down the sidewalk. In the other hand, she carries a large pitcher of iced tea. She is wearing a backpack, which contains packets of chicharrones and fried wonton wrappers. She sweats as she walks in the morning sun to Párraga's Casa Comunitaria, where she's launching yet another project called Breaking Routines.

Six women are waiting for her. She had hoped to attract many more. "So we're not an army," she says, loudly enough to get their attention. "We can still start here."

Breaking Routines is another dream of Argelia's. As she

settled into Párraga, she began worrying not only about the children around her, but also their mothers and grandmothers, all of whom are relentlessly oppressed by sexist men. "My blood just boiled," she says of watching these women get shoved into domestic servitude. So she went to Casa Comunitaria, a small local organization dedicated to cultural events, and persuaded them to let her host a new Afrodiverso program.

"Our goal is to help you quit cooking, scrubbing and ironing," Argelia announces solemnly. "We want your families to share the load rather than treating you like their slaves." Her audience, all of whom are over fifty, listen intently as she continues, "We may not have much, but we can still do a lot. We can celebrate, sing, smile, gossip, dance, talk freely. Anything that makes us happier contributes to our overall quality of life."

She goes on to tell the women that they should begin their day by leaving the house in the morning, rather than doing their chores. "Your husbands and children get dressed and go out," she notes. "Why can't you? Just tell them it's their turn to take care of the house." The women look at her, startled.

She goes on to explain how she supports herself, selling the same tea, chicharrones and wonton wrappers she has brought as snacks. She gets up at 6:00 a.m. to sell them on the street, which is hard, of course, but what she earns is hers alone. She's not dependent on anyone to take care of her.

Immediately, the women start talking with each other, as Argelia had hoped they would. Beatriz, fifty-three, says, "I need motivation like that. I came here because I'm running out of steam."

Miriam adds, "Argelia, your story really surprised me. I feel very moved. It's wonderful to see the world differently at our age. Where there's life, there's hope."

Lázara, fifty-eight, agrees. "For years, I've been cut off. I retired, and suddenly all I did was serve my family. It's selfish of them. We can't let ourselves stay isolated."

Argelia then tells the group, "We're going to work on empowering you, resisting gender-based violence, all of that. And we're going to do it through drag."

No one speaks. The women glance around. Some laugh nervously.

Argelia ducks out to go to the bathroom. Shortly after, a man walks in unannounced. He's wearing tight jeans, high-tops, a bright shirt, a hat and a chain. He introduces himself as Alberto, then launches into Argelia's favorite song: Alejandro Fernández's "Hoy tengo ganas de ti." She likes the line, *No hay nada más triste que el silencio y dolor*: nothing is sadder than silence and pain.

Later, Argelia will tell me that "Alberto empowers Argelia. He's a man in my life who has never hurt me, never damaged my self-esteem. We have to teach these women to understand that. Remember, by the time Alberto and I met, I could do carpentry, plumbing, electrical work. But he gave me courage."

FISHING WITH CONDOMS

Alberto isn't agile enough to hoist himself onto the wall of the Malecón like he used to. Instead, he leaves the climbing to his catlike eighteen-year-old son, Luis, who points at the wall and says, "I'll go up. You do the reels and the condoms down here."

Luis vaults onto the wall, where he begins stringing his fishing pole. Alberto, fifty-five, glances up at him, then opens the nylon bag and takes out three boxes of condoms, which he scatters at his feet. His son jumps down, the smack of his flip-flops shattering the quiet. He's brought along a bucket of water holding a very small barracuda—yesterday's catch—which he guts and cleans carefully before cutting it into small chunks. Beside him, Alberto inflates condom after condom. His hands and mouth shine with lube. He twines six condoms together into a star and passes it to his son, who attaches it to the line he's getting ready to cast into the dark sea.

It's 3:39 a.m. Other than the crash of waves on the reef, the city is silent.

* * *

Alberto and Luis live in a small house in Cerro. The area is several kilometers from the Malecón, but the two of them haven't missed a night of fishing here in two and a half years.

Every night around 10:00, father and son go to the bedroom, draw the curtains, and kiss Mercedes, Alberto's wife and Luis's mother, goodbye. She's very ill and eats hardly anything but their daily catch. Her doctors say she hasn't got long to live. "Life is cruel," Alberto tells me, leaning on the seawall. "One day my wife was the healthiest woman I knew, and the next she was sick. Our whole routine transformed. I had to quit my job to take care of her and to help Luis graduate. I wasn't letting him drop out of school."

From the top of the wall, Luis picks up the story. "I'd never fished before, but I couldn't let my dad go out alone every night. When I was still in school, I was just sitting at home, watching Mami and imagining what it was like for Papi out here. I wasn't sleeping or studying. As soon as I graduated, I said I wanted to learn how to fish." He's holding a hunk of Styrofoam, which he attaches the line to with a sailor's knot, letting the baited hook dangle while he wraps more of the line around one of his dad's condom stars. It's windy, which isn't good for casting. Luis lifts the rod without releasing the line, watching the condoms bob in the air. He seems to be at an impasse—the star is rising straight up over his head—but then the wind dies down. It's his moment to cast.

Alberto says, "It's not the only reason we use the condoms, but having them helps us tell which way the wind's blowing."

"We'd have no idea without them," Luis agrees as the line flies out from the pole. "It's too dark out here to see."

"Mainly, though, we use them as floats," Alberto adds, pointing at the star now bobbing on the water. "We use the condoms to tell us how far the hook's gone. Also, the air in them stops the bait from sinking too far. It jumps up and down between the surface and the deeper water, which attracts fish."

Alberto and Luis aren't the only ones on the Malecón tonight. Squadrons of condom stars drift on the water or fly in the air like kites. "I like that we do this together," Luis shares.

"Just me and my dad. We go hours without talking sometimes. We hear the sea speaking. Very early in the morning, we hear it sing."

"Our life's not easy," Alberto reminds his son. "We're earning our living and keeping your mother alive." He then tells me, "Luis and I have a deal: the biggest, most beautiful fish we catch is for Mercedes. We sell the rest in the neighborhood."

"Papi taught me to fish with condoms," Luis says, "and I'd have no idea how to do it without them When there was a shortage last year, we nearly had to quit."

Government statistics report that Cuban demand for condoms has spiked in the last few decades, rising to 5 to 6 million used every month. In 2014, when public pharmacies began running out, even *Granma* reported on their absence. *El Vanguardia*, a local paper in Villa Clara, urged residents of the province to use other forms of birth control, reminding them that "all efforts are worthwhile in times of scarcity" and adding that "the ancient Egyptians used knotted animal intestines to protect themselves."

In Cuba, a package of three condoms costs a peso, or one U.S. nickel. In order to end the shortage, the government earmarked $300,000 for buying condoms from an Indian company. The sum was twice the Ministry of Public Health's entire budget for that year.

* * *

"When I started learning to fish," Luis says, "the condoms grossed me out. I didn't like getting my hands slimy. I was sure we didn't really need them, but now I get it." He gives the rod to his dad and begins digging for more reels in his backpack. He repeats the process of stringing the line, but this time, he blows up the condoms himself.

"We get them in bulk," his father tells me. "We buy twenty-four packs so we don't have to go to the pharmacy every day." Before he can continue, he suddenly jumps, startled. Luis has punctured two condoms, which burst with sounds like gunfire.

* * *

"We're from Las Tunas, in Oriente," Luis explains. "We don't have relatives or many friends in Havana. If we're not here, we're taking care of my mom. When we had the party, it was just our neighbor and two of our fishing friends."

"Nobody knew that the balloons were condoms," Alberto brags. "Not my wife, not even the other fishermen."

Alberto and Luis threw a surprise birthday when Mercedes turned fifty-two. It took them a year of saving up: coming to the Malecón earlier and leaving later, borrowing a boat from friends on the weekends in order to catch bigger fish in the open water off Playa del Chivo. "We got more fish in a month than we had the whole time we've been coming here," Luis says.

Alberto tells me that "you don't need condoms when you're fishing at sea, but we used them anyway, for protection. It's so dark out there, and we're not very skilled. It was frightening. Imagine looking around—" he illustrates with his hands— "and seeing no light this way or that way. We did it for Mercedes, but we were glad to come back to the Malecón."

On Mercedes' birthday, Luis and Alberto came home at nine in the morning, sang to her, and then told her they had to go out. She had no idea what was happening later that day.

"We'd cooked some food the day before at our neighbor's house," Alberto says. "She's a first-grade teacher, and she gave us her watercolors."

While Luis went to the pharmacy for condoms, not wanting to dip into their fishing supplies, Alberto cooked with their neighbor and made paper chains out of old issues of *Granma*. When he got back, Luis cut open four plastic jugs and mixed paint in them: red, yellow, green and blue. He soaked the condoms in paint for half an hour, dried them off, and inflated them. "It was my dad's idea," he says. "We didn't know whether it would work. When we blew the first one up and it was green, he started to cry." Luis's eyes water at the memory. He stares out at the sea.

Soon the three of them were heading over to surprise Mercedes, the neighbor carrying two bags of food, Luis and Alberto, skin and clothes stained with paint, bearing the balloons. "I bet everyone thought we were clowns," Alberto remembers. "A pair of little kids came and begged us for the condoms, which they thought were balloons. We gave them one."

In the afternoon, the rest of the guests arrived. Mercedes got emotional when the group sang "Happy Birthday." That evening, once everyone had left, father and son cleaned up and helped Mercedes to bed. Luis tells me, "Right before she fell asleep, she asked, 'Luisi, where'd you get the balloons?'"

An hour after the party, Luis and Alberto were back on the Malecón, waiting patiently for a fish to tug on their line.

THE INFERNO

Nothing about Ariel Ruiz Urquiola's life is random. At forty-three, he feels not a trace of uncertainty. Stubbornness is his flag, and, marching beneath it, he's never had trouble deciding where to go.

Growing up, he wanted to be a veterinarian. He'd catch cockroaches and bumblebees, detach and inspect their antennae, and feed them to lizards, which he'd then trap and dissect. While his sister Omara built sandcastles on the beach, he collected algae and other forms of marine life, including, once, a Portuguese man o' war that burst in his hands, badly irritating his eyes.

Eventually his mother, Isabel Urquiola, now sixty-one, explained to him the difference between veterinary science and biology, which she taught at a primary school in the Havana municipality of Playa. On the weekends, she'd entertain her son with outings to the Natural History Museum, the zoo, the aquarium or the botanic gardens. Omara rarely wanted to go to those places, so Isabel acceded to her requests to also visit the national art museum.

Ariel would lose his temper when his sister flouted the laws of nature by painting a lion pink or green. Back in the 1970s, the Ruiz Urquiola siblings, like all Cubans younger than twelve, received three toys from the state every year. Each neighborhood held a lottery in which the children drew tickets from an enormous drum; later, their parents would take their children to a toy store to claim their rewards. The toys fell into three official categories: "basic," which was an expensive, useful item like a bicycle or stroller; "non-basic," which could be a doll or toy car; and "directed," which might be a top, a set of jacks or a bag of plastic soldiers. Drawing a number one in the lottery was significantly better than, say, a sixty-three, since the toys, which were imported from the USSR, came in unreliable quantities, and the lower your number, the better your odds of getting what you wanted most.

Ariel was always luckier in his draw than his sister. But although he often got low numbers, at some point in his childhood he began eschewing the more exciting toys in favor of the objects he needed to build what had become his favorite thing: a toy farm. The farm lived in his bedroom, where it grew year by year, until he had a herd of toy cattle, some geese, horses, multiple buildings, and, of course, a farmer and various farm hands. The farm also had its own train, a gift from his uncle, Armando Urquiola Cruz, founder of Pinar del Río's botanic garden.

Ariel and Omara usually spent their summer vacations in Mantua, Pinar del Río, at their grandparents' house. Along with one of his cousins, Ariel frequently accompanied his uncle on specimen-collecting trips to the nearby pine forest. By age ten, Ariel had his own herbarium.

* * *

"Ariel's a loudmouth now," says Elier Fonseca, a field biologist who teaches at the University of Havana, "but in college, he was even worse."

Fonseca has been Ariel's friend and colleague for more than two decades, since their undergraduate days. He recalls an ecology lab during their second year of school that required the two of them to kill a large number of lizards. Ariel stood up and declared that the methodology was wrong, unprofessional and deviant. His classmates stared in astonishment as he argued with the professor, both of their voices rising. At the end of their disagreement, Ariel spat, "Professor, this is a mediocre class." Fonseca explains that Ariel "has a tendency to speak in a way that creates problems and misunderstandings."

Although he encountered many problems and misunderstandings during his college career, Ariel managed to receive a BA in biology in 1999, earning high academic honors and an award for conducting the best research among his cohort. After graduation, he began working at the University of Havana's Center for Marine Research, studying turtles. His supervisor, Professor Georgina Espinosa, told Ariel that he had a doctoral student's command of the subject, so Ariel decided to get a PhD.

Ariel's doctoral work concentrated on Cuba's hawksbill turtle population, which led him to the discovery that the Ministry of Fisheries—which no longer exists—had legalized hawksbill fishing despite that fact that it was an internationally protected endangered species. At the time, Cuba exported hawksbill shells to Australia, England, France, the Low Countries, Scandinavia and Japan. The Cuban state justified the shell trade by claiming that the nation's hawksbill population was self-contained and in no danger of extinction.

"All lies," Ariel says. His research found that more than 70 percent of turtles captured in Cuba had migrated to the island. He also discovered that in Nuevitas, a port city in Camagüey, the Ministry of Fisheries had begun falsifying its turtle studies by "going to a beach, killing a young turtle, and sending a lot of samples of its flesh to our lab, marking them as different turtles so that our results would show that all the turtles caught in Cuba were born here." Ariel explains that the government gained financially from the hawksbill trade, which was not only a violation of international endangered-species protection agreements but also flouted Cuba's own law reserving turtle meat to feed the nation's children and the elderly. His investigations demonstrated that no childcare center, clinic, school or retirement home had received a single piece of turtle meat.

Ariel and his working group brought their findings to a marine turtle conservation conference in Baja, California. Their presentation included a plan to launch a public awareness campaign to save Cuba's hawksbills. It would be the first program of its kind on the island since the Revolution. Naturally, the scientists at the conference were appalled, and various international organizations reacted so swiftly that within two days, Cuba had called a halt to all turtle fishing. However, instead of being celebrated, Ariel returned home to discover that he'd been suspended from his doctoral program. He only got to defend his dissertation and graduate in 2008, after a formal appeal to the National Commission for the Academy of Sciences. He dedicated his dissertation "to the cause of the impossible," and wrote in his introduction, "Biodiversity is as important to wild animals as freedom of thought is to Homo sapiens. An H. sapiens unable to think for himself is the victim of life's circumstances. Self-awareness liberates him."

* * *

After earning his doctorate, Ariel was told that he could continue at the Center of Marine Research as long as he didn't study any other species that were significant to Cuba's fisheries.

So he began studying the genetic code of mollusks in the Sierra del Infierno, a project that earned him a grant from Berlin's Humboldt University. Working with Professor Espinosa, he launched a collaboration with the Leibniz Association, a German group of nearly 100 independent research institutions. The Cuban government, having not forgotten what had happened with the hawksbill, erected many barriers to impede his work. Although his project eventually became impossible to carry out properly, Ariel's research still earned him the respect and admiration of his German colleagues, who recruited him to a position at Humboldt.

Dr. Alexandro Rodríguez, who teaches biology at the Free University of Berlin, says that, "[p]eople were constantly offering Ariel permanent jobs in Germany, but he always wanted to go back to Cuba." Rodríguez himself earned his undergraduate degree in Cuba in the late 1990s, but he left for Europe immediately after that, which is where he reconnected with Ariel. In Germany, he shares, "Ariel lived very frugally. He socked away every euro he could for the farm he was going to start in Viñales." Dr. Rodríguez would drive Ariel to the airport for his visits to Cuba, the trunk of the car stuffed with suitcases filled with farming implements: "I used to tease him for being so cheap, but I admired him, too. Nobody else was hauling that kind of thing home."

* * *

When Ariel was in fifth grade, his mother noticed that his usually pale skin was getting tan, as if he were going to the beach. One day, she went unannounced to his school during an exam period, and, when she looked in his classroom, she saw that Ariel wasn't there. "I found him on the playground," she tells me, "in the hot sun, sitting at his desk with his test. He'd been punished for telling the teachers not to cheat. He was against them whispering the answers to the students, so he got banished outside." Stories like this show how, even at a young age, Ariel already had his maternal grandfather's moral code engraved into his consciousness.

Ariel began helping his grandfather sow rice and beans with his ox cart in Pinar del Río when he just six years old. His sister Omara explains that "our grandfather was a Mason. He was always opposed to the government's ideas, though he wouldn't say so aloud. We understood it based on his upright behavior, his refusal to give in to abuse or corruption. He was an enormous support for our family, and his ethics influenced us, my brother especially."

Ariel's grandfather spent a year in prison after a fellow Mason asked to borrow two horses, one for himself and one for a friend who had participated in the armed counterrevolution in the Escambray Mountains after Castro took power. The man had fled to the United States, but had returned to visit Cuba; he was now trying to get to the western coast to escape. But the government was onto him, and he and the other man were both captured. One of them mentioned Ariel's grandfather's name during his interrogation, and so he was arrested for conspiracy. According to Omara, she and her brother only "found out about the political incarceration [of their grandfather] because of our father."

Their father, Máximo Omar Ruiz Matoses, a seventy-one-year-old former army official, now lives in Spain. A radar and telecommunications engineer, he ascended to the rank of lieutenant colonel while leading a technological development group that, per Omara, "bought all of Cuba's espionage equipment: scanners, walkie-talkies, you name it. He was the one who discovered and started interfering with the U.S.'s propaganda broadcasts."

However, by the end of his career, Máximo had become a dissident within the Ministry of the Interior. At Party meetings, he railed against the conduct of its leaders. He was especially disappointed about the scandal surrounding Arnaldo Ochoa, a general who was executed in 1989, along with three co-conspirators, for treason and drug trafficking. "After that," Omara explains, "my father put in his retirement papers. He asked to meet with Raúl Castro before he left to talk about the distribution of resources."

Máximo was assigned to be a border guard while awaiting his retirement. Days after his transfer, he was arrested and charged with attempting to leave the country illegally, behaving dishonorably, contempt, espionage and desertion. Omara points out that "my dad used to travel to Japan with millions of dollars in a suitcase to buy technology. If he'd wanted to desert, he'd have done it then. None of those accusations had any basis." She adds that, "when the government especially wants to wound us, they say he worked with Ochoa, which is a lie. He had no connection to that man."

Máximo Omar Ruiz Matoses ended up spending seventeen years in prison. "We've paid a price for being his kids," Omara says.

* * *

Omara Ruiz Urquiola is forty-five and teaches at Havana's Higher Institute of Design. She's had health problems for some time. In 2004, she found a lump in her right breast. Her brother, through a friend, got her a consultation at the National Institute of Oncology and Radiation, or INOR, where a doctor and two medical students examined her, did a biopsy and said, "Well, if your water goes out, you don't have to look far for an emergency supply. You've got water cysts in your breast."

A year later, the lumps had gotten bigger. Omara's breast ached when she drank coffee or ate chocolate. Her nipple leaked blood and amber liquid so often that she began putting a cotton ball in her bra. Her brother, recognizing the gravity of these symptoms, got her an appointment at the Center for Medical and Surgical Research, where the head of chemotherapy, Dr. Catalá, tested the liquid and told her he was going to start her on "a little bit of prevention" the next day.

In the morning, Omara sat in the waiting room, surrounded by women who'd lost all their hair while Ariel spoke privately to Dr. Catalá. She remembers her brother opening the office door, standing on the threshold and asking, "Are you ready to fight?"

Now, twelve years later, Omara tells me, "It was only then that it hit me: I had cancer."

"You're not going through this alone," her brother told her, "but it's going to be hard. You have to swear to me that you're going to try to live."

Omara began her "little bit of prevention," which turned out to be her first cycle of chemotherapy. Meanwhile, Ariel began to study his sister's illness. He looked at her mammogram and CT scans, which indicated that there was hope: the tumors hadn't spread beyond her breast. She says, "He'd get up at 5:00 a.m., bring me breakfast in bed, and make sure I was comfortable before he left for work. All day long, he'd call and remind me to eat. In the evenings, he made me dinner. I had to go through six rounds of chemo, and I had to keep my strength up."

* * *

One night, Ariel recalled a presentation he'd heard in college about a tree in the Amazon whose sap contained a cancer-stopping chemical so potent that the indigenous population of the area hardly ever got cancer. He discussed this chemical with Dr. Catalá, who told him that taxanes, the drugs derived from the tree, were so costly that Cubans couldn't obtain them. Ariel used every connection he could to get Omara the drugs, which he brought to the clinic. However, Dr. Catalá refused to give them to Omara, saying, as she recalls, "that it wasn't worth giving such expensive medicines to a woman who had three months to live. He recommended moving me to palliative care instead."

On hearing that, Ariel stood and hissed, "As a doctor of biology, I have a duty to leave with the patient right now."

"You're no doctor," Catalá said.

Ariel shot back, "Neither are you."

Ariel brought Omara back to INOR, where she resumed treatment, receiving both the taxanes and cobalt radiation therapy that shrank her tumor to within the recommended surgical margins.

The only issue now was that the waiting list for an operating room was three months. Desperate, Ariel reached out to Dr. Miguel Fleites, INOR's former chief of surgery, who'd been fired for speaking out about irregularities in the treatment provided by the agency. Dr. Fleites examined Omara in his home and concluded that immediate surgery was necessary, as in three months, the tumor was likely to have grown beyond the surgical margins again. He persuaded a friend to loan him a surgical room at the Hospital Manuel Fajardo, where he operated on Omara's right breast; five months later, in another borrowed room, he operated on the left breast.

* * *

In 2016, the Swiss pharmaceutical company Roche sent the Cuban medical import/export company MEDICuba a shipment of a targeted breast-cancer drug called trastumazab that was about to expire. When the medication arrived, the doctors at INOR rejected it on safety grounds. While MEDICuba hunted for a replacement medication, Omara and her fellow patients missed two months of chemotherapy. Because of the delay in treatment, Omara ended up with cancerous growths on her skin and lumps in both of her reconstructed breasts.

Ariel appealed to INOR to help his sister and the other patients who needed trastumazab, but got no response. He then decided to go on a hunger strike. Omara came home from teaching a design class one day and found a note that read, "Omi, I've found a solution to my uselessness and frustration: I'm starting a hunger strike in front of INOR's chemo wing, and it won't stop until I see you getting treated. I don't know how long this will last. I hope to see the other side. I don't want anyone from our Δ near me. Your chemo is my goal." The Δ represented their family triangle: two siblings and their mother.

Ariel's hunger strike was met with police beatings and three brief incarcerations. After he was released from prison for the third and final time, the medication finally arrived in Cuba. Omara tells me that "it's in short supply again, but I always have what I need. Other patients don't, but the institute sets some trastumazab aside for me."

Oscar Casanella, an INOR biochemist and friend of the Ruiz Urquiolas, says that "Ariel has one regret in life: bargaining to get his sister's treatment. He agreed to stay quiet as long as she gets what she needs, and now other patients get nothing."

* * *

Fog sits thickly over the Viñales valley, the hilltops emerging like reefs from the sea. Roosters crow, waking the other animals who live at the Inferno, Ariel's farm. The name is a joke, as well as a reference to its location in the Sierra del Infierno, 300 meters above sea level in Pinar del Río.

Ariel bought a house here in 2015 and negotiated the rights to enough land to create an agro-ecological farm, which sits inside Viñales Valley National Park, a UNESCO World Heritage Site.

Ariel designed his farm as an ecological and phylogeographical laboratory. His central goal is to intelligently breed native flora and fauna in order to repopulate the area. He began his work the same year he was fired from his job at the Center for Marine Research, allegedly for "inter-institutional fraud" re: the research plan he was meant to carry out in Germany. In reality, he lost his job because of his rebellious obstinacy and criticisms of the state. "Punishing people like Ariel is a security measure," Oscar Casanella explains. "Ariel is dangerous enough on his own. Imagine if there were a gang of them."

Having been ejected from Cuba's scientific institutions, Ariel has dedicated himself to sustainable agriculture. Yosvani Chávez, one of his neighbors in the Sierra del Infierno, says that "he's done a great job here. I was born in the Sierra, and it wouldn't occur to me to do all the stuff he's done. He's got fruit, coffee, animals—and he does it all on his own."

Before Ariel came along, the land on which the Inferno sits was a wilderness. Now it's a paradise where cows and horses wander into Ariel's doorless house and hunt for snacks in the kitchen, and ducks, chickens, guinea hens and geese amble around freely, mobbing anyone who crosses their turf. Cuban trogons, the evasive national bird, sit in the pines, around which grow seventeen varieties of banana, purple and green king grass, as well as Valencia, blood and navel oranges, yellow papayas, sugarcane, mamey, caturra and robusta coffee and Antillean mahogany trees filled with grafted fruits.

* * *

As if the Inferno weren't enough, Ariel also combats ecological crimes and violations in Viñales Valley National Park He denounces poaching and wilderness tourism and once gathered up eighty illegal traps in a single day. His activism, however, annoys the local government as well as many of his neighbors. For example, one of his neighbors lets his hogs destroy Ariel's crops and contaminate the water on his land. A man hunting hutia, a large indigenous rodent, once threatened Ariel with a gun when Ariel attempted to stop him. Groups of tourists steal his fruit. Four of his cows have been killed, and he once found one of his mares with gashes on her back and hindquarters. When the Sierra got electricity, it didn't come to the Inferno, which is powered by a lone solar panel.

One morning, Ariel and his hired hand, Joseilis Varela, were mending fences when two forest rangers showed up, asking to see the paperwork sanctioning their repairs and possession of power tools. While walking to Ariel's house to look at the documents, the rangers began arguing with the biologist, who criticized them for never responding to his complaints. One of the rangers opened his pants and began to urinate on the ground, which infuriated Ariel. He started recording the interaction on his phone and demanded their names, referring to them as "rural guards," which is an insult: before 1959, that was the name for the oppressive police forces in the Cuban countryside.

The rangers arrested Ariel for "contempt of authority," and he was taken to jail at the police station in Viñales. After being held for five days, during which time he was deprived of the right to communicate with his family, Ariel was finally allowed to meet with his lawyer, Amaury Delgado. A summary trial was held only a few hours later. "I didn't get to shower or brush my teeth," Ariel says. "I got handcuffed, thrown in a cop car, and taken to court." His lawyer didn't even know what the charges were until the trial began.

"It was absurd," says Elier Fonseca, who attended the trial. "Surreal. Completely for show. Nobody had a shred of evidence against him."

Nevertheless, a judge in Viñales's municipal court sentenced Ariel to a year in prison for disrespecting the rangers. He was initially incarcerated in Pinar del Río. When word of the case spread outside Cuba, Amnesty International declared Ariel a "prisoner of conscience." Heather Nauert, a spokesperson for the U.S. State Department, demanded his freedom, as did Luis Almagro, secretary general of the Organization of American States, and the Catholic Church in Cuba.

A month after the trial, Ariel was transferred to the Cayo Largo penal colony, where he was denied the right to work in the prison. As a result, he launched another hunger strike. Omara wasn't allowed to communicate with him, but on her forty-fifth birthday, she got a call from another prisoner who read her a note from her brother. It contained the phrase, "Freedom or nirvana."

After sixteen days, Ariel was moved back to the Pinar del Río prison. However, instead of an ordinary cell, he was placed in solitary confinement, with no light or fresh water, in a rat-infested room so small he could only lie down at an angle. He continued to reject food and water, and after six more days, he was handcuffed and taken to the Provincial Hospital Abel Santamaría for rehydration. Although the nurses were kind to him, the guards taunted him with food, threatened him with violence when he returned to prison, and refused to admit visitors. Ariel's only weapons against this harsh treatment were Vipassana meditation and the continuation of his hunger strike.

Eventually, after two months of not eating, the prison system's medical commission released Ariel to serve the remainder of his sentence at home.

* * *

"I was looking for pain relief," a very frail Ariel tells me. He's just gotten out of prison, and his head is still shaven. He coughed as he spoke and needed a cane to steady himself when he rose from his mattress on the floor of his sister's bedroom. "This was from years ago. My hip was bothering me, and I had a limp that came and went. No one understood it: not orthopedists, not physical therapists, nobody."

Ariel, who'd regularly ran ten kilometers after work when he lived in Germany, was frustrated. Four years ago, he learned about Vipassana, which he explains was "described to me as a technique for diminishing pain," He and his cousin, Armando, the one with whom he'd collected plants as a boy, traveled to Germany for a Vipassana course which turned out to be a ten-day silent retreat. Speech was forbidden except with the master, and only when the master chose to. Meals were sparse: just fruit, vegetables and liquids, no dairy or meat. Ariel explains that "Vipassana is based on the breath. In the course, we took it twenty-four hours at a time. For the first three days, you listen to a recording. Your thoughts distract you, jump all over, take you back to your childhood, turn into nonsense." As he spoke, he sat in his meditation posture, legs crossed in a butterfly shape. His spine is straight, his hips relaxed, his gaze forward. "A lot of people quit," he continues. "I shared a room with four people at the start of the course, and by the end it was just me. When you're there, you sleep from 11:00 p.m. to 5:00 a.m., and the rest of the time, you're either meditating on a mat or walking through the forest, which you can only do at midday, and only if you don't talk to anyone while you're out there."

On the fifth day of the course, Ariel's emotions overwhelmed him. He began weeping uncontrollably, an explosion of tears. "I couldn't stop crying," he remembers. "I couldn't meditate, couldn't reach any kind of equilibrium. My head was totally empty."

When his teacher saw him sobbing, she asked, "What country are you from?"

"Cuba."

"As of today," she said, "you'll get extra food."

On the tenth day of the course, the students who'd stuck it discussed their experiences. Ariel's teacher introduced him to an Israeli girl who'd also broken down on the fifth day, saying, "some people's origins mean they come with a much deeper history of suffering than the rest. Usually, our students' issues are just heartbreak or rejection."

After the teacher left, Ariel asked the girl, "What did she ask you when she saw you crying?"

"'What country are you from?'" the girl answered.

* * *

Today, Ariel seems agitated, unlike himself. As we drive out of

Havana, where he has been recovering from his hunger strike, he is silent.

Omara and I join him in the back seat of the yellow cab. Isabel, their mother, sits up front. She has devoted her life to her children. After her divorce in 1980, she decided never to saddle them with a stepfather. Omara told me, "My brother was high maintenance. You couldn't just plop him in front of some cartoons."

But Ariel was also the man of the house, even when he was a boy. He was mason, carpenter and plumber; he regularly joined his grandfather when he was slaughtering livestock so that he could help out and then bring home the meat. Isabel rotated between the classroom and the kitchen, where she made sweets and croquetas to sell. She mended clothes and cleaned houses, but still, during the Special Period, Ariel had to drop out of college to help support her and Omara. He worked at the zoo until a professor found him a grant to re-enroll in the biology department. "We were a trio," Omara tells me, "a triangle. He still feels responsible for us."

In the cab, the driver breaks the silence. He's from Pinar del Río, he says, and goes to Viñales all the time to hunt birds. "I like to get those little blackbirds."

A smile appears on Ariel's face. "Not blackbirds," he says, "Melopyhhra nigras, native to Cuba and Grand Cayman. I have a farm, and if I see you hunting those birds on it, I'll run you off my land." He then turns his face to the window, seeming not to notice a government billboard that promises Efficiency and Reliability. "See those barrel palms?" he asks. "Native to Western Cuba. All our biggest ones have been logged. It's a travesty."

We pass another billboard advertising Unity and Victory. Ariel tells the driver, "You know, there are prettier birds here than the blackbirds. On my farm, I see the great lizard cuckoo, which I love. I also see a different kind of blackbird, a more common one, called Ptiloxena atroviolacea. They're wonderful birds, but Cubans don't respect them."

Another billboard announces, *Patria o Muerte*: We Will Win. Beside it are uprooted trees. "Teaks," Ariel says. "You can see they're full of termite holes. A waterspout must have passed through here."

CYBER SOLDIERS

It's Saturday afternoon, and Rodríguez is drinking rum in his living room, wearing only a pair of shorts. He's watching a live broadcast of Barcelona playing Real Sociedad with his cousin and a couple of friends. Not far from the television is a wooden table with a bottle of Havana Club 3 Años, some cut-crystal glasses, a can of Coke, a plastic plate of chicharrones and two packs of Popular cigarettes, the ones with filters.

Messi scores for Barcelona. Moments later, the table starts to dance. Rodríguez's phone is vibrating, shaking the bottle and glasses, though the chicharrones don't move. He grabs the phone and looks at the screen, and his face changes. He goes onto the balcony and, after a brief conversation, heads directly to his room and emerges in a shirt and trousers.

"Going somewhere?" his cousin asks.

"Work," Rodríguez says. "Somebody wrote an article online that shit talks Fidel."

* * *

Rodríguez is not his real name. Although he never wears a uniform, he works in a policing capacity in a department at the Ministry of the Interior that he prefers not to identify, though he will say it is "dedicated to monitoring Cuban cyberspace." He explains further that, "we don't attack or hack anyone's site or account. Primarily, we keep an eye on what people say about Cuba online, gauge the consensus, and, if it's overly negative, we strike back."

Every day, Rodríguez and his fellow cyber soldiers search and scan the outlets that are most outspoken or "subversive" in their coverage of Cuba, checking a list that includes blogs; foreign media; the underground and opposition press; and people of interest on "insidious" social media platforms. Rodríguez has three Facebook accounts: a real one he uses to keep in touch with friends who've emigrated, and two fake ones "for defending Cuba from anyone who denigrates the Revolution."

Maimir Mesa, Cuba's Minister of Communication from 2012 to 2018, said in a parliamentary debate that "the online sector should be developed as a weapon in defense of the Revolution, guaranteeing security from risks and threats of all types." He added, "In order to achieve this, we must implement an action group within the national security system, a task force that can perfect the required process."

According to Rodríguez, "denigrating the Revolution" can take many forms. It can mean "negative posts about a government measure or project such as urban transit; publicly criticizing a government figure; or writing anything in favor of the United States." He has two fake Twitter accounts, one on Instagram, and an unused one on Google+. He says that "I'm less active on social media than my subordinates. Most of them maintain several accounts and post constantly. It isn't only replying. We try to show what Cuba is, our achievements as a nation, and not just wait for somebody to start baiting us." How many subordinates does he have? He won't say.

Lázaro Benítez, an official at the Ministry of the Interior, states that "our cyber soldiers are performing one of the country's most important missions. We can't allow ourselves to be penetrated on the battleground of the internet."

* * *

In addition to the Ministry of the Interior, nearly every state institution helps police Cuba's cyberspace, adding online "combat" to their employees' other roles.

Sonia Cot, a former employee of the People's Supreme Court, helped found the court's cyber brigade. "We had a meeting to decide who had the knowledge and political skill to clean up the image of Cuba's courts and justice system online," she tells me. Her group selected judges for the mission, then recruited tech-savvy young people to get them online. She says, "we'd write reports on the negative things we found and how we responded. I'd never realized how many lies people tell about Cuba."

The same process occurred at the Ministry of Public Health. Ricardo Gálvez, an anesthesiologist at the Hospital Calixto García, says that starting in 2017, "all employees have been informed that the state requests our assistance in resisting the online counterrevolution" He's talking about a document issued by the Ministry's director of communications, which was meant to be internal but got leaked to the press. It declared that the "mission of activists and cyber soldiers is to be on the alert for any news spreading on the web that could affect the Revolution."

Another one of the cyber soldiers' tasks is to spread positive ideas about the Revolution through online debate. "We're refuting slander," Rodríguez tells me, "but also supporting citizens and helping them avoid statements that could be misconstrued. No one wants to show the enemy their belly."

Rodríguez engages in this project mainly through blogs, though of course he doesn't write under his real name: "Between our forces and the rest of the institutions that lend a hand, we have scores of voices in the blogosphere."

* * *

Although it's summer in Cuba, Rodríguez is never without a coat. He ties it around his waist or across his torso. Presumably his office is cold. He describes it only as a "computer lab," adding that "it isn't the country's only one."

Raiko Hernández, a member of Federacion Estudiantil Iniversitaria, or FEU, an organization formed in the 1920s in response to corruption in the Cuban academic system, verifies this. Hernández graduated in 2012 from the University of Informatics Sciences (UIS), founded in 2002 as part of a political campaign Fidel called the "battle of ideas." Raiko tells me that "our course of study includes trolling. It's not an assignment so much as a special request from the administration."

Alina Enteza, also a UIS graduate, has taught there for two years. She explains that "our university is in charge of one of the most important battles of our time. Cyber soldiers are Cuba's new revolutionaries." While the UIS's physical campus is deteriorating, Raiko says that in his five years as a student there, "we had it all: food, computers, nice dorms. We got to play on the internet, and so we did anything we were asked. We had our own laptops, good Wi-Fi, and instructions to post good things about Cuba for an hour every two days, and argue with anyone talking shit. It was supposed to be a military operation, but for us, it was a game."

UIS has 10,000 students, whose job is to create software and information technology. Learning by doing is paramount. All over campus are computer labs with high-speed connections, but, Raiko says, "we couldn't go in all of them. Some are just for professors and Party officials. I heard the Ministry of Communication developed its guidelines for cyber policing in one of those labs."

Not long before I spoke to Raiko, the legendary singer-songwriter Silvio Rodríguez wrote the following on his Facebook account: "I lost access to the internet yesterday afternoon. Coincidentally, my record label, Ojalá, heard from the Ministry of Communication yesterday that we have been selected for an inspection. We will be hearing from the Integrated Revolutionary Organization. I hope to keep you all informed." He later added, "My loss of connectivity was due to a broken cable that's been repaired. As to the inspection and the cyber police, we'll see..."

* * *

Before he became President of Cuba, Miguel Díaz-Canel, then the First Vice President of the Council of State, said in a discussion on technology and the computerization of the country that "the enemies of the Revolution are conspiring to portray Cuba as a country disconnected from the global internet." It was an old-school declaration, mired in the linguistic muck of rhetoric that is often characteristic of Cuba's politicians. It was also a denial of the reality: per the United Nations, Cuba—an island of 11.2 million—was, in fact, mainly disconnected. At the time, only 4 million Cubans were able to use the internet, and only 7.1 percent of the population could do so at home. And yet Díaz-Canel maintained that "the nation's connectivity has grown 346 percent, which proves our advancement on this front, despite many complications."

He wasn't fooling anyone. His 346 percent number came from the creation of more than 630 computer labs and 370 public spaces with Wi-Fi—all real, but everyone knew that when you go from having nothing to having some scraps, the data looks impressive, but nobody's life is transformed. All that changed, in this case, were the numbers, which the men who rule Cuba got to brag about in their speeches and reports.

* * *

In a nation where the average reported annual salary is 740 pesos, or $30 a month, and an hour of internet access costs $1, Rodríguez is required to report monthly to his superiors on the online voices and outlets that do most harm to Cuba's image, as well as the topics his brigades of cyber soldiers promote online. "Our work," he says, "is to keep #Cuba trending—which it always is—and ensure that the hashtag gets support." He chooses not to clarify what else is involved in his online battle, in which he uses all the power the state has given him to mercilessly surveil the unwitting people who must count out every cent of their wages to ensure that they have enough to eat, live, and, now, get online.

THE HOLE

"Where do you live?" the first cop asked.

"Over there," Raudel, nineteen, replied, pointing at a scrubby stretch of huts.

"You know you can't be here," the second cop said. "Not while there are tourists around."

"But I live here." Before the cops came over, Raudel had been sitting on a high oval rock, drawing circles in the wet earth with a twig.

"Show me your papers," the first cop demanded.

"I don't have them on me. I don't have an address, anyway. My neighborhood doesn't have streets. No name, either. People around here call it 'the hole.'"

"Well, we already told you that you can't be here, so we're going to have to bring you down to the station."

Sun radiated from the police car's white paint. Clouds stalled overhead. As the car started, Raudel, alone in the back, twisted to look at the twenty-one-foot bronze Che Guevara looming behind him. Carved under the statue was Che's most famous phrase: *Hasta la victoria siempre* ("until victory, always.")

* * *

Only "the hole's" inhabitants call it by that name. No one else calls it anything. Officially, it doesn't exist. It isn't on the maps that divide the province of Villa Clara into municipalities. According to the 2012 census, "the hole's" inhabitants don't exist anymore than their neighborhood does, as they are not listed among the 833,424 residents of Villa Clara, 210,220 of whom live in Santa Clara, the provincial capital.

A poor shantytown beside the Plaza de la Revolución in Santa Clara, "the hole" is only a block long. It's a slum hidden by trees and shrubs that sprout from the cracked dirt. It has no streets, only a muddy trail that winds through the tall grass from shack to shack. No one in "the hole" has an address, which means it's impossible to get mail. Public Services doesn't come to collect the trash or trim the trees, so the neighborhood's electric lines are constantly getting tugged down by overgrown branches, which means that the few residents who are lucky enough to get to listen to the radio or watch television at home are often subject to days-long power outages. Legally, the power company can't respond, since "the hole" doesn't exist. For the same reason, its inhabitants can't build or request houses.

Bad times arrived in the neighborhood in 1987, the year the Plaza de la Revolución was built. Villa Clara's government declared the area surrounding the plaza a "protected zone," which meant that everyone who lived there did so illegally. Only the three houses constructed before 1987 are allowed. Those houses are made of brick or cement, while the rest, the "illegal" ones, are built of wood and soggy cardboard. Remberto Suárez, a functionary at the Ministry of Construction, tells me that the Cuban state considers it an extralegal act to "establish, occupy, or cohabitate in dwellings in a protected area." Laws against anti-social conduct forbid the people who live in "the hole" from entering the Plaza de la Revolución, which is how Raudel, mere meters from his home, got arrested for harassing tourists.

* * *

"We have no means of communication," Carlos tells me, balancing his bulk on an old stool. "No phone service at all. It takes balls to survive here."

Carlos has the nicest house in the neighborhood. Not only is it made of brick, but it also has more than one room. When it rains hard enough for the hungry mud to start sucking down people's homes, or when there's a hurricane or cyclone, Carlos opens his doors so that his neighbors can shelter in his house until conditions improve. Among them are Teresa, sixty, and her twenty-nine-year-old son. When the weather is bad, Teresa arrives in a wheelchair pushed by her empty-eyed son, whose murmurs no one can understand. Her house has no water, and she has little faith in the rotting boards of her roof.

Teresa is in renal failure. She has one kidney, and its function is declining fast. Every time Carlos sees her she's frailer, quieter, less present. Her son has a congenital disability I don't ask about. He struggles to say a few words in a row, and yet he somehow manages to cross the city daily to collect food from the school where his father used to work as a janitor. When his mother is sick or has a doctor's appointment, he pushes her across the city, over two kilometers, from their nameless neighborhood to the hospital.

In 2004, before he fell picking coconuts and died, Teresa's husband petitioned the state for funds to construct a safer house. The only reply the family received was the assignment of a social worker, Yusmany, who visits twice a month. "I'm not a miracle worker," Yusmany tells me. "I do what I can with the resources I'm given. I understand the difficulty of their situation, but you do have to remember that they're illegal."

Teresa and her son have one source of income: the 242 pesos—not quite $11—a month they get from her late husband's pension.

* * *

A man who refuses to give me his name—he was in jail once, he says, and is concerned that speaking to me could cause him trouble—invites me into his home, which is full of nylon. Scanning his collection, he tells me that people here gather it to waterproof their homes.

He's forty-nine and has lived in "the hole" for forty years. "I cleared this land to build a house for my family," he says. "So far it's fallen down twice."

A few days ago, he got good news: the state is giving him 160 square meters of land and 1875 pesos, or $78, to build a new home. He should receive both in seventy days.

After prison, he's only managed to work on agricultural crews that pay poorly; he refuses to tell me how little he earns.

Outside his house are two dogs who just gave birth. He has pigeon coops on his roof.

* * *

"He's the reason the government wants to demolish our houses," Ramón says, looking at the statue of Che Guevara while wrestling a nail out of a board in the dirt entryway of his home.

Ramón, fifty-five, lives with his wife Gladys, forty-one. On his left wrist is a Seiko watch. His right hand is missing the index and ring fingers. Gladys wears an exceptional amount of costume jewelry. Aside from frying pans and kettles, the only items of value in their house are an old Sharp tape recorder and an Atec-Panda television with a piece of bamboo for an antenna.

"I don't go to meetings anymore," Ramón says. "All they do there is lie." He is referring to his time as a member of the Communist Party. "But no one can take my ideas from me," he adds, "and no one can drag me into that opposition shit."

Ramón is a professional stonemason. He's spent his life working on mosaics and tile. In the early 1980s, when the province began building the Plaza de la Revolución, he was one of the workers they hired. "Who would've guessed it would put us in this situation?" he says. "We get sick because we don't have running water. Cars can't get in. We don't have phones. If we enter the plaza we get kicked out for harassing tourists. And now the government says they can't help us because we're living in a protected area."

As Ramón wages war against the nail, he sings a Mexican song, *Tenía un chorro de voz y ahora queda solo un chisguete*: "I used to have a stream for a voice, and now all that's left is a trickle."

GAME OVER

José and Leo are out of bed at 3:35 in the morning., ready to start their day. They're dressed in dirty shirts and drab army pants, though José is wearing leather boots that go up to his ankles, while Leo has on tall plastic rain boots. Yawning, they emerge from their apartment, wind their way down the curving staircase of their colonial building in Old Havana, and head out to get the cart from which they'll sell fruit, vegetables and dry goods for most of the day and into the night.

At this early hour, Havana is a somnambulist, a strange, empty, spooky city very unlike the one most Cubans know. Mysterious shadows and murmurs are everywhere. Boulevard San Rafael, which, within hours, will be a rushing river of people coming and going, buying and selling, is a long, gaping passage, the cracks and holes in its asphalt exposed. The only signs of life are a cat pawing a chicken carcass in a bag; three women; two parked pedicabs; a handful of old cars for hire that no one is currently hiring; and a police cruiser slipping quietly off to the Prado.

José and Leo take Calle Bernaza to a parking lot holding pedicabs and pushcarts. An old man opens the gate, and they pay him five pesos and thank him for watching their cart. The rusted wheels shriek unbearably as they depart into the quiet darkness.

For the next sixteen hours, José and Leo won't be separated from the cart. The two will eat breakfast beside it in a cheap café, munching on dry bread with under-seasoned picadillo and a sliver of melted cheese. For lunch, they'll each have a bowl of whatever José's girlfriend has cooked for them. Water comes from dirt-covered jugs they keep in a wooden vegetable crate; bathroom breaks are at job centers, where they have to ask permission to go. At 8:00 p.m., they'll say goodnight to the cart, having pushed its 600-pound weight some six kilometers, and head home to shower, eat, and go to bed so that they can start again tomorrow.

* * *

Play. Level 1.

Twenty-five minutes after leaving their house, José and Leo arrive at the Calle Egido wholesale terminal market, where the majority of Havana's street vendors purchase fruit and vegetables to sell. Legally, the market isn't permitted to sell to them; the only sanctioned wholesale hub in Havana is El Trigal, on the outskirts of the city. But by 4:00 a.m., the Egido market, which is blocks from the Capitol, is practically an agricultural fair. An insatiable mass waves cash in the darkness, winding between columns, relying on headlamps, cell phones, and the delivery trucks' yellow headlights to see. Surrounding every truck is a crowd haggling with the entrepreneurs who, money belts slung over their torsos, announce how much a crate of this or sack of that costs. A pair of cops stand by, witnessing the spectacle,. "All they have to do is nod, and everyone's so scared they give them a cut," José says.

At the back of the market is a ramp where the trucks wait to enter. Here, farmers begin selling their goods, shining flashlights around like miners. Nearly everyone has an eastern accent. A narrow passage runs from truck to truck all the way through the market. It's jammed with loaders who earn their living hauling produce from the market to the pushcarts.

José, who owns the cart, goes into the market to shop. Leo waits outside, guarding the cart and arranging goods on it as the loaders emerge with José's purchases. Once José is done, the two of them leave, passing a line of vendors waiting to do the same thing they just did.

* * *

Pause.

In 2010, the state issued a list of sanctioned forms of self-employment, one of which was selling fruits and vegetables on the street. The idea was to help citizens purchase produce without having to travel to a market.

According to tax data, Havana has 1777 legal street vendors. It has many unlicensed ones, too. José got his license in 2011 to help out a friend who had quit selling food. "He wasn't good at mornings," José says. "He hated having to get up." José eventually decided to start his own business. He purchased wood and poles from a carpentry shop, "liberated" some tires from an ancient Soviet motorcycle sidecar, and built his cart, which, he says, "is one of the nicest in the neighborhood. I take good care of it. See how well the bearings distribute the weight? You get some real Frankenstein carts around here."

Leo, on the other hand, has no license.

* * *

Start.

The return home is much slower than the departure, as it's not easy to push the cart. Even with both of them pushing, the cart groans slowly forward, its wheels complaining about the

600-pound load.

By the time José and Leo reach their apartment, it's five in the morning. Yesterday's unsold food comes downstairs; the food they bought today to sell tomorrow goes upstairs. All the produce, especially the dirt-caked yams and taro roots, needs to be cleaned. Dividers are placed in the cart to separate tomatoes from peppers; two-peso guavas from three-peso ones; plantains from burro bananas; eggplants from cucumbers; onions from scallions. José hangs small nylon bags on the side of the cart; he sells them to customers for a peso. Leo complains about cleaning the yams, as its getting his shirt muddy. José says they have to do it as a courtesy for their customers.

* * *

At 6:02 a.m., they have their first shopper: a woman in her forties who's an economist for the state. She picks out some guavas, saying she's on a new diet. As she walks away, gray water splashes from somebody's window into the street. Havana is starting its day.

* * *

Level 2.

All the shadows have disappeared. Sunlight now illuminates the overgrown old buildings. People are everywhere, and the city is loud. José and Leo's morning shift is well underway, with business heating up steadily.

"You can do this some of your life," José says, "but not all. It's too hard for how little you make."

Pedestrians hurry by, all of them glancing at the cart. Even those who don't slow their stride, who have everything they need in their pantries and refrigerators, take a look. Cubans can't help it. We've gone hungry long enough that nothing interests us more than food. We work to eat, live to eat, dream of eating. We're constantly asking ourselves where our next meal will come from.

A man stops and asks how much for a guava. When Leo tells him, he picks up a three-peso one, examines it, squeezes it, and then throws it on the ground, where it explodes like a grenade, splashing my shoes with juice. "What's wrong with you?" the man shouts. "Where do you get the nerve?" Leo gets angry, but José intervenes quickly. As the man walks away, he declares, "Fidel did this to us."

Everyone complains about José and Leo's prices. Even those who don't buy anything call them gougers and cheaters, accuse them of getting rich off the people's backs. José tells me, "I get it. Wages are low and prices are high. But what can I do? I buy as cheaply as I can and sell for just a little more that I earn. I'm in business here. If the state could bring costs down, shoppers wouldn't get angry at me."

José is used to the insults; Leo, not so much. José is calmer, more phlegmatic. Leo is the opposite: hyperactive, without much patience for the customers.

A woman asks how much for tomatoes and onions. She inspects them, scowling her opinion of the price. Suddenly she launches into a discourse on the penny, which is hard to find in Cuba, but still important, she says, since in other countries, you can charge $9.99 and why not here, why don't José and Leo have one-cent coins, it's ineptitude, naivete, under capitalism nobody would shop at their cart, and they'd starve. Leo gets angry again, and José intervenes again. After the woman finishes her rant, she turns her back and marches away.

Pause.

* * *

José wanted to attend college, but only made it through high school. "My parents couldn't even have bought me shoes for college, let alone paid for the rest," he says. Before becoming a street vendor, he worked as a carpenter's assistant and did computer support in his neighborhood, but he says that "some weeks I had no work, nothing in my pocket. I couldn't contribute at home, so I switched to selling food."

José pays Leo $4 a day to assist him. Leo is from Manzanillo, in the southern province of Granma. He would prefer more reliable, less grueling work; he's sick of living on José's couch, getting up at the crack of dawn to haul crates of vegetables—of "feeling like a slave," as he puts it.

Leo, who's twenty-six, leaves his home province for seven or eight months at a time to work in Havana. His parents split up when he was six months old. His father took the bed and Leo's crib when he left—"revenge because my mom didn't want him"—and Leo never saw him again. Eventually his mother found a new partner in Havana, and the three of them migrated to the city. However, when Leo was fifteen, his stepfather threw him out of the house without telling his mother, and so he had no choice but to go back to Manzanillo. There, he enrolled in technical school, studying economics. For three years, he ate nothing but bread and the meals a neighbor gave him on Sundays. He'd leave school in the afternoons and haul sand or brush until he'd earned enough to pay for the next day's bus fare and food. "At graduation," he recalls, "everyone was celebrating with their parents. I was third in my class, and when I crossed the stage no one congratulated me but the dean. I didn't have a single relative there."

After graduating, he worked at various odd jobs: janitor, gardening, and working for a friend's masonry company. Eventually, he set out for Havana. "What else could I do?" he asks. "Nobody can live on a government salary." He's considered suicide, he tells me, but he's too cowardly. He'd do it if he could take a drug strong enough to just shut his eyes and, without pain or suffering, end his "miserable life."

Leo recently had surgery for a hernia and appendicitis. After his operations, he was "not supposed to do hard labor, but I've got to earn a living."

But that's not his biggest concern. Instead, what upsets Leo the most about his situation is that he's covered in mud all the time. "What Havana girl's going to want me like this?" he gripes. Despite his appearance, not a single woman passes the cart without Leo catcalling to her.

* * *

Start.

Sales start to decline around noon, so José breaks out his more seductive pitches. "Come see this gorgeous tomato, ma'am, worth every cent;" "Sir, we've got all you need, anything, the customer's always right;" "Auntie, how's it going? All well in the neighborhood?" By this point we've walked several blocks, dodging the sun and the state inspectors, who live to harass pushcart vendors. Arguments between the two groups are constantly erupting on street corners and in alleys.

By lunchtime, we've landed beside the house where Manuel Sanguily, one of the heroes of Cuba's nineteenth century war of independence, was born.

* * *

Level 3.

Agriculture on the island has long been mismanaged, yet the state has chosen to scapegoat pushcarts as the reason for rising grocery prices and declining crop production, even though they're the smallest link in the chain.

During a parliamentary debate on the subject, Raúl Castro ordered Marino Murillo, then the Minister of Economy and Planning, to "put an end to food inflation."

"Mr. President," said Murillo, "we're going to take care of it."

From that day on, street vendors became a target. Obtaining a new license became impossible, and those who already had one had to pay the state 150 pesos a month (up from 70 pesos.) Cops and inspectors hounded the vendors constantly, swarming the streets, which became full of decommissioned carts and abandoned merchandise. Though some people demonstrated against this harassment, the vendors' encounters with authority only grew worse. Before long, the vendors started to hide from the inspectors.

"It's like a video game," says José. "You're constantly scurrying around the corner just so you can do your job. If you get caught, you lose your money." The inspectors once stopped him three times in a single day. "It's amazing how worthless a license is," he tells me. "Even if you've got all your papers, they just invent a reason to make you pay. I've gotten thrown on the ground before the inspector even asked me for my license. It's insanity. Instead of helping you, the state beats you, picks at you, tries to get you to quit. A lot of the old guard's given up."

* * *

A married couple, A and B are former pushcart vendors who'd rather not use their real names. Having given up their cart, they still sell some produce from home, under the table, to support A's mother, who's missing a kidney, and stepfather, who's housebound.

During their final month of legal street vending, they received two 1000-peso fines for conducting sales while standing, instead of walking. "It was like dealing with the Mafia," B says loudly, hands slicing through the air. "None of the inspectors care if you have a license. You get taxed illegally, and if you want to hold onto your cart, you have to give them cash and food."

Pause.

* * *

Nex to a bodybuilding gym in Old Havana, at the corner of Calle Sol and Calle Cuba, is the agency that inspects street carts.

At noon, the lobby of the building is dark, and there is no guard or receptionist. I arrive, look around, and then walk in without anyone stopping me. On my left is a small patio crammed with decommissioned pushcarts waiting to be stripped apart. On my right is a warren of bureaucrats at their desks. Only one, a quiet, mixed-race man, is male. All the others are Black women wearing Santería bracelets and gold necklaces.

One has a gold tooth. Her name is Yeney—she won't share her last name. In fact, her name and a pair of photos of the posted regulations for street vendors are all I can get from her. She won't divulge financial data, discuss the inspectors' treatment of street vendors, tell me what directives the agency gets from the state, or acknowledge the collapsed pushcarts eavesdropping on our conversation.

Miguel Sánchez, an inspector I meet on San Rafael, is chattier. "Every month," he explains, "we're given a certain monetary target, and we try our hardest to reach it. If we don't issue enough citations, we don't get our bonuses." Of the crusade against pushcarts, he says, "At the beginning of the year, we were told all of them had to go, and we carry out our orders. Half of them are unlicensed, you know."

In order to prevent corruption, inspectors switch areas weekly, and partners monthly. Sánchez tells me that "some of my colleagues are bad at their jobs, but I wouldn't say I've seen any corrupt ones, personally."

* * *

Start.

As the afternoon wears on, José and Leo cross paths with a vendor who is different than most of the others. He isn't wearing boots; his clothes are clean; and his cart is nearly empty. He has on a snapback, giant sunglasses, and several nickel chains. Asked about inspectors, he says, "My cart's a hustle. I sell foreign women bananas for a dollar each. I just work in the historic district, and there's no inspectors there, just girls."

* * *

Alfredo Wilson is from Peru, but he's lived in Cuba since 1991. He runs a farming co-op in Caimito, and hates the pushcarts. He says that the vendors aren't interested in quality, just money, and so they sell rotten produce. Last avocado season, Alfredo fed his pigs three months' worth of avocadoes rather than sell them to street vendors at cost.

As a rural laborer, Alfredo earns less than anyone in the agricultural chain. "I sell my tomatoes for two or three pesos each," he says, "and in the city, they go for ten." He tells me he initially wanted to live and farm in Mali, but had to leave the country due to war. After that, he thought Cuba seemed like the ideal place for cooperative agriculture, but it turned out that he was wrong. "Country and city are out of sync," he says. "We have to grow it out here—you can't produce enough in the city—but the rural orange growers can't even afford a glass of juice. No wonder no one wants to farm. Prices are going up because we live like serfs in the country."

* * *

Level 4.

By nightfall, José and Leo are practically collapsed on their cart from exhaustion. During their sixteen-hour workday, they've circled the same streets over and over as the city slept and stirred, then quieted again; they've hidden successfully from inspectors; and they've sold a lot of fruit, some vegetables, and not many of their dry goods. Now the sun is sinking into the port, and it's time to go home.

People are still moving like ants down the narrow streets leading from the Capitol to the sea, but by 7:47 p.m., the mimes and jugglers and picturesquely skirted, cigar-smoking women are gone. The pigeons have flown up to church cornices and abandoned buildings to roost. José and Leo trudge hone with their cart. By now, it's closer to 300 pounds than 600, but it feels twice as heavy as it did this morning. Its wheels shriek like an injured animal, the sound mixing with a legendary *son cubano* melody that three old men are playing on guitars at an upscale bar full of tourists.

NOT ANOTHER DAY

It was midday, and Elia Felipe still hadn't seen her son, Arturo. She knocked on his bedroom door in the garage where he lived, but he didn't answer. She tried to open the door, but it was locked from the inside. She went to the patio and called through his window, but, again, received no reply. Met with silence, she lost her composure; next door, Raúlito heard her shrieking, "Help! Help! Help!"

Raúlito, a former neighbor, had arrived in Havana several days earlier from the United States, but hadn't yet seen Arturo, a childhood friend. He had tried to visit him a few times, but on each occasion, Arturo, without leaving his room, had told his mother, "Say I'm not seeing anybody. Not him, not anyone else."

Upon hearing Elia's cries, Raúlito hurried over. "Arturo isn't letting me in, and I'm frightened," Elia told him. Raúlito managed to force the door open, where he saw Arturo Martínez-Escobar, age fifty-one, dead, having hanged himself with a rope.

Elia Felipe is eighty-three now. Quietly, she remembers, "I didn't look. I didn't want to see him that way, but now it weighs on me that I didn't have the courage. I should have gone in there." We're in her kitchen on Quinta Avenida in Playa, Havana. Her only son took his life seven years ago.

* * *

Someone dies by suicide every forty seconds. According to the World Health Organization, 800,000 people take their own lives every year. Seventy-five percent of suicides occur in low- and middle-income countries; the highest rates, measured in suicide deaths per 100,000 residents, are in the former Soviet countries Lithuania, Russia and Belarus.

In Cuba, suicide is the tenth most common cause of death. In 2018, the Ministry of Public Health's annual statistical report found that 13.3 out of every 100,000 Cubans died of "self-inflicted injuries," and that 1493 Cubans—1186 men and 307 women—had died by suicide that year. Havana had the most suicides (181), followed by Holguín (173) and Villa Clara (164). If you look at rates rather than numbers, though, Villa Clara's is highest (21 for every 100,000 residents of the province), followed by Sancti Spíritus (18.2), Artemisa (17.3) and Matanzas (17.3). Suicide is the third most common cause of death for Cubans between the ages of 10 and 19, after accidents and cancer, though only 1.8 of every 100,000 Cubans that young dies by suicide. Among Cubans ages 15 to 49, it's the fourth most common cause of death, after heart disease and, again, accidents and cancer.

Back in the 1950s, the island had the world's highest suicide rate, with 340 suicides for every 1,000,000 inhabitants. By the 1960s, the rate was 15.4 for every 100,000; by the 1970s, it was up to 19 for every 100,000, peaking at 23.3 in 1982. Four percent of the country's deaths that year were suicides, a number alarming enough that the government created the National Suicide Prevention Program. Initially, the program's mandate was to identify at-risk groups and individuals, but it was changed at the start of the twenty-first century to focus more on community action.

* * *

"A person can be completely all right one day, and then the next, something unleashes disaster within them," Elia Felipe says. She lives alone in her old age, along with three dogs and a cat. She has short hair and two birthmarks on her wrinkled face. She walks with a cane for balance.

She tells me that Arturo's troubles began in the 1970s when he was a university student in electrical engineering. At the end of his freshman year, he was about to hand in an exam when a classmate asked him for help. Arturo wrote the answers on a piece of paper, balled it up, and slipped it to the other student. A few days later, both boys were called into a disciplinary hearing for having given precisely the same answers on the exam. Rather than just suspending them, the committee expelled both young men from the engineering school. The expulsion completely changed Arturo's life.

When Elia came home that afternoon, her son's door was half-open. She went into his room and found him unconscious on the ground, his wrists bleeding. With a neighbors' help, she got him to the hospital in time to save his life. "Getting expelled from college after freshman year was traumatic," she remembers. "He couldn't take it. But if it hadn't been the expulsion, it would've been something else."

Although the Ministry of Education offered Arturo the option of going back to school in another discipline, he refused. For six months after his suicide attempt, he didn't leave the house, and though he eventually received psychiatric treatment, Arturo nevertheless sank into a profound depression.

* * *

Elia Felipe had a friend who taught theater at the University of Arts, and she asked them to help Arturo enroll in the department.

He took the placement test, passed, and went to classes for two weeks. It seemed like he might be getting his life back on track, but then a hurricane hit the island, closing all the schools for a few days. When the University of Arts reopened, Arturo didn't want to go back. "I could tell he was still fretting about his old school," Elia Felipe recalls. "He felt guilty. He thought he'd brought shame on himself."

After that, Elia Felipe decided to give her son whatever he wanted to try to keep him from spiraling. She and her second husband, Mario, supported Arturo and his girlfriend, then wife, to whom he was married for ten years. Mario, who died in 1997, had come on the scene when Arturo was a child. Arturo's father died when the boy was seven. He was a military officer and shot himself in the head.

* * *

"Suicide is preventable," explains Dr. Sergio Pérez, sitting in an armchair in his house in the eastern city of Bayamo. Pérez, sixty-six, is an international authority on the subject, and is a member of the Suicidology section of the World Psychiatric Association. Outside his house are signs that read, No to Suicide. Yes to Life. "Suicide is a cause of death just like a car crash," he says, "but we have a way of treating it as if it were its own phenomenon. Usually, the motives are similar: problems in the family, problems in love, though it varies from culture to culture." He says that what matters most is getting to the person in time to ask what Dr. Pérez calls the lifesaving question: Do you want to kill yourself? After that, you need to work out how complete their plan is: "A person who's really set on suicide will know how, where and when, not just why."

With a patient who's reached that point, Dr. Pérez's initial goal is just to keep them alive until the crisis ends and their suicidal intent starts to lessen. "A crisis is brief," he states. "You can't point a gun at your head for eternity. Either you put it down or you shoot." But, he adds, the psychiatrist "can't get a savior complex. We can't keep everybody alive by ourselves, which is why it's important to help families intervene. No one dies by suicide when other people are around."

Dr. Pérez is retired from his medical practice. "If you want to see me," he says, "you can send me a message or come to my house." He hung up his white coat after two cases that pushed him to the limit. In one, a woman came to him saying that she was concerned that her mother was depressed. "Bring her in right away," Dr. Pérez told her. "For all we know, tomorrow's too late." He diagnosed the mother with severe depression and sent her to a psychiatric hospital. A week later, he ran into the daughter on the street, who told him that her mother had killed herself the day before. "We went to the hospital," the daughter explained, "but there wasn't room for her, so we were sent home. I went out for a minute to buy meat, and when I came back, she'd hanged herself."

In the other case, a man with a severe mental illness came to Dr. Pérez' in crisis because his wife had left him. Pérez sent him to the hospital with orders to admit the man immediately. Not long afterward, he ran into the ex-wife and mentioned that he'd had her husband hospitalized. "I know," the woman said. "The hospital monitored him overnight, decided he was okay, and let him go. He went straight out to buy pills and killed himself."

* * *

"Growing up, Arturo didn't know that his father had killed himself," Elia Felipe says. "He just knew his dad was dead.

Somebody told him the truth when he was an adult. It wasn't me."

Elia Felipe never imagined during her ten years of marriage to Arturo's father, who was also named Arturo, that one day she'd open the door to a man who had come to tell her that her husband had shot himself. Arturo, Sr. was thirty at the time, a lieutenant in a covert group in Cuba's internal security ministry. A colleague of his was the one who "stood on the doorstep and gave me the news. It was horrible."

According to Elia Felipe, her husband's work was classified, but involved "enemy forces," and that one of his group's responsibilities was providing arms and personnel for Che Guevara's ill-fated Bolivian mission. Arturo, Sr. worked with Patricio and Antonio de la Guardia, a pair of brothers who were eventually found guilty of treason. Patricio spent thirty years in jail; Antonio was sentenced to death by firing squad.

"Arturo's dad was never involved in his life," Elia says about her husband's relationship with his son. "He came home once every two weeks. He never played with him." As a result, Arturo wasn't particularly upset when his father died, though the loss did lead him to develop a close bond with a neighbor named Cesar. Elia recalls: "Once I heard him tell Cesar, 'My dad died, so now you have to take me to get my haircut and play soccer with me.'"

* * *

Elia Felipe was twenty-one when she fell in love with Arturo, Sr. Once they started dating, though, a problem quickly arose: while each of their families loathed Castro, Arturo was in the army, and he was a loyal soldier. Thus, the new couple were rejected by both families. Elia was kicked out of her house because of the relationship, and since she was unmarried at the time, she had to ask her father if she could move him with him, although she'd never actually met him. "My family wouldn't let me get to know my dad," she explains. "As far as they were concerned, he was the world's biggest villain. My mom married him when she was fifteen and got pregnant right away, but after I was born, he confessed to her that he was gay, that he'd only married her for appearances. My aunt found out and made my mom divorce him. For twenty years, they kept me away from him."

Elia knew that her father was an accountant for a men's grooming product company, so when she needed a place to live, she got in touch with him. Without hesitation, he agreed to take her in—"which," she says, "kept me out of prison." She continues: "At the end of 1959, my aunt hid some counterrevolutionaries, and when they got caught, she was sentenced to thirty years in jail. My mom was investigated, too, and even though she was innocent, she spent six months in prison before they decided not to bring any charges."

* * *

Elia was all alone when she gave birth to Arturo. Her father and now husband were working; her mother-in-law disapproved of her; and her mother had gone to visit her aunt in prison. Elia left the hospital with nobody to help her hail a taxi or cook her something once she got home. "My maternal grandfather would've been there for me," she says. "He was the one person in my life who always stuck by me. But he was the first suicide in my family."

* * *

Outpatient treatment centers are the base of Cuba's public

mental health pyramid. In these centers, teams of psychologists, psychiatrists, social workers, therapists and nurses handle an array of occupational, individual and group therapies.

I visited a treatment center in Havana twice a week for a month. Since the Ministry of Public Health bans the employees of these centers from communicating with members of the independent press, I will not identify the institution, or the people who I spoke with.

"We see patients Monday to Friday, from 8:00 a.m. to 2:00 p.m.," a psychiatrist told me. "Other doctors and clinics refer them, but all of the patients come voluntarily. Usually, they need daily help to recover stability, and so if a patient misses a day, we call them. If somebody stops coming altogether, though, we have to close their case."

A fifty-two-year-old patient who has survived two suicide attempts told me his story in a day room. "I have a real problem," he began. "What happened was that I was taking pills, and my family took advantage of the situation to get me to sign over my house to them. I cut off contact with them and moved in with a friend, but I felt completely alone. My life seemed meaningless. Then my friend went out of town, and I fell apart. I wasn't eating, wasn't showering. I scratched my skin until it turned into little balls. I shut the windows in my room for weeks. I'd watch TV in the living room at night, then go back to my bedroom when the sun came out.

"I got to the point where I was shitting and pissing myself. I was nearly dead. I even called a friend, a different one, and told her, 'I've given up.' After that I got a knife and held it to my throat, but that cold metal, no. Shit, no. I wasn't strong enough for that.

"My friends took me to the Hospital Calixto García. I wasn't better at first. I still didn't eat. I couldn't stand up. But eventually I got strong enough to creep off to the bathroom with a sheet. I was tying a noose in there when a nurse saw me.

"What I want now is to get rid of this problem. Coming to this center has helped me see that my life isn't meaningless. Improving it is its meaning. I'm one of twenty-five patients here, and we do therapy Monday through Friday, plus a cultural activity the center organizes every Wednesday to get us out into the city. We work out in the mornings. We play chess, or Parcheesi, or dominoes, just as a way of hanging out. We do group therapy, too, which is when we all talk about one person's problem. Helping each other shows us how we can help ourselves."

One of the psychiatrists at the center takes me into her office and clicks around on her laptop, pulling up a PowerPoint for a class she just taught on suicide. Before showing it to me, she says, "You know, Cubans have very quick tempers. It's a national idiosyncrasy, but it's changed our whole history." Of the nation's suicide rate, she says, "It's connected to substance abuse among young people. Alcohol is especially bad, but marijuana, even though a lot of countries are decriminalizing it, is most correlated with mental illness. It's especially connected to schizophrenia, which is as big a challenge in psychiatry as cancer is for doctors treating the body." She explains that "any disconnection from reality can make depression and suicidal thoughts worse," and calls the former "the illness of the twenty-first century. Supposedly everyone has at least one major depressive event in their life now."

* * *

The General Calixto García University Hospital is Havana's most centrally located medical center, which means that many of the city's residents go there when they are having an emergency. The hospital also has a behavioral health unit that offers psychiatric and psychological services. Dr. Israel Fagundo, head of the unit, tells me that the patients who come here suffer from "schizophrenia, bipolar disorder, drug and alcohol addictions, hallucinations, delusions, psychosis and disassociation from reality. I treat patients who've heard voices or seen visions telling them to kill themselves." When I ask Dr. Fagundo what drives the majority of Cuban suicides, he explains that "suicide never has a single cause. Often, it has to do with personality type more than anything else. Highly impulsive people are at risk, and people who do poorly with frustration. Of course, so are people who inherit mental illnesses like depression or bipolar disorder. And then we worry about loneliness and family dysfunction: domestic violence, alcohol or drug addiction in the home, any history of abuse."

Before he became Calixto García's head of behavioral health, Dr. Fagundo was a consultant psychiatrist at the hospital. His role was to liaise with his colleagues treating suicidal patients in other departments. If, for instance, a patient arrived in the burn unit having attempted to self-immolate, the doctors there would stabilize the person, then call Dr. Fagundo.

He was in that role for six months before the hospital asked him to take over the behavioral health unit. On accepting the job, he made a number of changes. "I switched to a community mental health system," he shares. "It's an understanding of psychiatry developed in inpatient British treatment centers in the 1950s. Once a week, the unit's residents lead a meeting, and everyone comes: their relatives, their care team, anybody involved. It's one of our techniques for building solidarity and acceptance among the patients, but it also helps create a therapeutic community in which we're all equal. Patients get to give doctors feedback, demand what they need, protest bad conditions. We're here for them, in the end, and they deserve autonomy, input and influence."

The meetings are recorded. Afterward, Dr. Fagundo studies the footage. "I'm analyzing the patients," he says, "looking at their body language and their behavior as well as listening to them. I'm doing the same with the doctors, including myself. It's the best way to improve the care I provide."

* * *

Dr. Fagundo did his psychiatric residency in Holguín, where he grew up, after serving in an international medical brigade in Nicaragua. With the money he'd earned in Nicaragua, he bought a Soviet-made car that was constantly breaking down. He always used the same mechanic, who eventually became his friend. The man was thirty-five and married, with two children.

One night, after Dr. Fagundo got home and changed out of his scrubs, his family told him that the mechanic's sister had called. It was 11:00 p.m., and the doctor thought it would be rude to call her back so late. In the morning, he went to work as usual. When he came home that night, there was another message: "Your mechanic's family called again. He shot himself."

"I had this sinking feeling," Dr. Fagundo remembers. He roamed around his house, asking himself over and over, "Why didn't that piece of shit talk to me? Why would he do a thing like that?" Apparently, the mechanic's fourteen-year-old son had stolen a significant amount of money from his aunt, the mechanic's sister. By the time the family discovered what he'd done, the boy had spent the money, and the mechanic couldn't repay his sister. After several days of stress and fighting, the mechanic called some cousins in the country and told them he was coming to visit; he had something he wanted to discuss.

The next morning, he and his son drove to the cousins' house, but after saying hello, the mechanic said he wanted to take a spin around the farm. He drove to the edge of the property, shot his son in the head, and then did the same thing to himself.

Dr. Fagundo pauses. Choking up, he says, "my heart rate's up." After taking a breath, he goes on, "It wasn't like he was unstable, or mentally ill, or depressed. He was impulsive, which is immensely dangerous. I can't come up with another reason he'd have done that. Just impulse and disorientation and shame that he couldn't pay the money back. Also, once somebody comes up with plan, the plan takes over.

"It was very painful for me to go to his funeral," he adds. "I was feeling a lot of remorse."

* * *

Elia Felipe was born in Punta Brava, which is outside of Havana. Growing up, her house had a large patio with a hut in the corner. The hut had originally been an outhouse, but now it was where the cleaning supplies were kept.

After sweeping the front walk one afternoon, Elia went to put the broom back in the hut and saw that the door was ajar. She pushed it open and saw her grandfather hanging from the ceiling. She was fourteen, and had never seen death before.

In a letter, her grandfather wrote, "Don't blame anybody for my dying. I'm tired of living, is all." But in truth, his daughters, Elia's aunt and mother, had been lobbying to move out of rural Punta Brava and into the city. At the age of sixty-four, their father wasn't prepared to leave the town where he'd spent his whole life. His arguments with his daughters about where to live poisoned the atmosphere at home. "I'm pretty sure he chose to die so that his daughters could move," Elia says. "It broke my heart. He was the center of my universe. He was the one who understood me, talked to me, walked me to school in the morning and waited for me in the afternoon." After her grandfather died, Elia and her mother and aunt immediately moved to Havana.

Elia couldn't have known at the time that her grandfather's suicide wouldn't be the only one she'd survive. "It's happened two more times," she says, "always with the most important person in my life. I don't know how I've hung on myself. Any one of them could have destroyed me." After all three deaths, Elia went through periods of overwhelming lethargy. It was as if she was paralyzed. She couldn't eat, read, go out, watch a show. Any activity was unbearable. "But it always passes," she says.

* * *

Elia Felipe did have a few years of peace during her son's marriage, until the relationship fell apart. Arturo's wife wanted to have a baby, but he refused, fearing that his mental illness was hereditary. She divorced him and, shortly after, found a new partner and got pregnant. For Arturo, this sparked a crisis. Against his mother's will, he sold his half of their house and moved into the garage. He began going out constantly, and before long, he'd been ravaged by alcohol and drugs. During the last months of his life, Elia would crisscross the neighborhood hunting for him. Sometimes his friends brought him home on their shoulders. "He didn't want to be alive," Elia says. "Not the way he was. He wished he'd lived differently, but now his existence was a burden. He was in his fifties, getting old without a purpose. He began to have these outbreaks of rage, and seizures from mixing alcohol, drugs and prescriptions—which didn't help him, and neither did any of his shrinks. He was disgusted by himself, but he couldn't seem to change anything."

The only change he made was to stop going out. Without warning, he isolated himself in his garage room, getting high all the time. He only emerged to say to Elia every morning, "Well, Ma, it's another day."

"He wanted to die," she says, "and in the end, he did it. I can't imagine how hard it was to live that way. It hurt him so much that he got kicked out of school. It dragged him down. It made him feel worthless."

Elia had Arturo's body cremated. She scattered his ashes on a beach full of stray dogs where she used to go swimming with him. She still swims there every day.

* * *

A year ago, Elia came home and, while removing her wet bathing suit, noticed a lump in her right breast. She went to an oncologist who, after the exam, asked, "Have you lost a son or daughter?" Some doctors, she later learned, believe that the death of an only child causes cancer in the right breast. Elia Felipe was diagnosed and, a few months later, had a unilateral mastectomy. During her treatment, a doctor told her that, "Suicide isn't just about the person who dies. It's about the people closest to them, too."

Recently, Elia watched a state television broadcast of *The Garden of the Finzi-Continis*, a 1970 movie in which a young boy dies. His funeral scene ends with a shot of his headstone, which reads, *Your parents thought to love you always, not to mourn you.*

When Elia saw that, she didn't cry.

A HOME FOR AFRIK3 REINA

Yenisleydis is thirty years old. She's single, Black, a rapper and poet. However, only her relatives call her Yenisleydis—the rest of Cuba knows her as Afrik3 Reina.

In 2021, a group of Afrik3's friends living in exile launched a crowdfunding effort on her behalf. At the top of the still active GoFundMe page it says, *A Home for Afrik3 Reina and Her Son*. The page features a large black-and-white photo of Afrik3 holding her three-year-old son, Nayad. She's beaming at him, and he's grinning at the camera. The fundraising plea below the photo reads in part, "Afrik Reina, a member of the San Isidro Movement, an artist in Spoken Word and a single mother, has been forced to move at least seven times in the last two years due to harassment by state security, the repressive arm of the dictatorship. The artist and activist has denounced her situation and the desperation in which she finds herself on social networks, especially for her three-year-old son, whom she cannot provide security or stability for, just for raising her voice against the oppression that she has experienced on the island." Within a month, the page generated $4,279 in donations. Afrik3's friends hope to reach $6,000, enough to pay for a small house on the outskirts of Havana where she might finally be able put her head down on a pillow every night and sleep beside her son without worrying about having to pack up and move the next morning.

Over the past two years, Afrik3 Reina has moved from Central Havana to Marianao; from Marianao to Vedado;

from Vedado to her home province of Mayabeque; and from Mayabeque to Cerro, all thanks to Cuban state security. Like other activists, independent journalists, and members of the political opposition—all of whom are, according to the government, mercenaries paid by the CIA or other foreign governments to "undermine the Revolution"—Afrik3 Reina has been forced to continuously relocate. If a friend or landlord lets her stay in their house or building, the state will charge them with supporting her supposed covert activities and prosecute them accordingly. As a result, Afrik3, like other dissidents who oppose the regime, not only lives in fear of going to prison, but is continually anxious about becoming homeless.

* * *

When Nayad was one, Afrik3 decided that she needed a stable environment in which to raise her son. She'd heard that in Miramar, the richest neighborhood in Havana, dozens of families had moved into abandoned homes. Rather than kick them out, the authorities were turning a blind eye, not wanting the independent press to start writing about the presence of squatters in a wealthy part of the city.

Afrik3 Reina spent four days prowling Miramar, but couldn't find a single vacant property. At the time, she was renting a little place in Vedado, but the owner—spurred by state security—had decided to sell the building, which meant that Afrik3 had to leave.

Having struck out in Miramar, Afrik3 moved one neighborhood over, to Kohly, where she found a gigantic house, built in the 1950s. She pried the door open with a knife and, upon entering, found an elderly woman already living there. The woman said that she'd started squatting in the house months before and that, though it appeared abandoned, it belonged to the University of Havana, which was not only letting her stay, but had set up a partition inside the house to mark off her space. Essentially, their message was: Be quiet and we'll let you live here.

Afrik3 lasted a week in the house. Her guess is that the neighbors heard Nayad crying and called the police, who came one afternoon and banged on the door. Afrik3 leaned out a window and called out, "I'm one of the many mothers in this country who doesn't have a home for her baby."

"What about the baby's father?" one of the cops asked.

"He doesn't have one."

Before the conversation could continue, a man appeared, surrounded by state security agents, and announced that he was a university administrator. One of the agents asked Afrik3 to let them in. She refused. "You have two choices," the agent said. "You can come out, or we can drag you out."

Before Afrik3 could reply, a woman emerged from the crowd, presenting herself as state security's head of political conflict. She said, "If you make us drag you out, then your son will be taken into custody by the state, and you're not going to get him back." Afrik3 opened the door.

She was taken out of the house and put into a police car, Nayad in her arms, and driven back to her apartment in Vedado. The owner wouldn't let her in, but the agents didn't have anywhere else to take her. Afrik3 and her son sat on the stairs outside the building for twenty-four hours until a women who lived there took pity and invited her in. "I owe that woman my life," Afrik3 says.

For two weeks, Afrik3 and Nayad lived with the woman and her husband, though Afrik3 was so afraid of upsetting them that all she did in the apartment was sleep and shower. She spent her days in parks or at bus stops, or walking around looking for a new home, only returning to the apartment when it was time to give Nayad his bath and put him down for the night.

One day, as Afrik3 was knocking on door after door in Central Havana in search of a room for rent, a car braked in front of her so abruptly that she tripped over her stroller, where Nayad was sleeping. She glared daggers at the driver—and then recognized him as one of the state security agents who'd kicked her out of her squat. He was watching her, and he wanted her to know it.

* * *

Afrik3 Reina's life changed when she met the artist Luis Manuel Otero Alcantará. "He helped me get bitten by the activism bug," she tells me. A friend introduced her to Luis Manuel and his former partner, the art historian Yanelys Núñez, and the three of them hit it off. Before long, they were an inseparable trio.

A few months after meeting Afrik3, Luis and Yanelys told her they wanted to create a Museum of Dissidence, dedicated to the memory of those who'd opposed the powers that be in Cuba. Afrik3 hadn't been politically active before, but the idea of the museum got her thinking, as did the shifts occurring in Cuba at the time. For decades, the Cuban state had crushed non-governmental organizations and other social groups, curtailing any possibility of societal change. But the reopening of relations with the United States, combined with a wave of social reforms including the right to private property and internet access, were shaking things up. Suddenly a new version of civil society was not only emerging but gaining strength, powered largely by the internet. Online, a new cohort of independent journalists and outlets arose, joining forces with social media to show ordinary Cubans aspects of their island that had long been obscured. No longer did the state have a monopoly on information. As this new reality emerged, so did a generation of young dissidents, including Luis Manuel and Yanelys.

* * *

While Luis and Yanelys were helping to transform the political landscape in Cuba, Afrik3 had to return to Mayabeque. She'd gotten pregnant, and the father wanted nothing to do with the child. According to her gynecologist, it was highly unlikely that she'd get pregnant again, and she didn't want to miss her only chance to be a mother. Still, the responsibility of single parenthood was "like a blackout," Afrik3 says. She needed her family's support, which meant she had to move back home. "It took me a long time to be ready to try Havana again," she tells me. "I had to deal with the emotions from my pregnancy. I wanted to concentrate on myself and Nayad."

While she was in Mayabeque, the government canceled the 2018 Havana Art Biennial. Luis Manual reacted by organizing the Alternative 00 Havana Biennial, which featured 100 Cuban and international artists showing their work in galleries and independent spaces across the city. For Luis Manuel, this was the point of no return. He had become a high-profile target, and state security began to harass him day and night.

* * *

When Nayad turned one, Afrik3 decided to come back to Havana. Luis Manuel and Yanelys got her diapers as a welcome present. In her absence, they'd bought a house in San Isidro, a neighborhood in Old Havana, which they wanted to transform into the base of an artistic movement whose goal would be "changing things in this country." Luis Manuel told Afrik3, "I hope I don't need to tell you that you're a part of it."

The San Isidro Movement was born.

The Movement introduced itself by fighting against Decree 349, which legalized artistic and cultural censorship. The members of the Movement presented demands to the Ministry of Culture; set up meetings; planned events that would flout the decree; and helped independent galleries present shows whose content flew in the face of regime-approved art. Their campaign ended up being so successful that the government had no choice but to cancel the decree.

For the new civil society, this was a massive victory. For the government, not used to defeat, it was an affront not to be taken lying down. As a result, celebrations of the decree's failure were repressed, and since then, the state has considered the persecution of artists and activists central to retaining power.

Unsurprisingly, the members of the San Isidro Movement were among the regime's main targets. State security subjected them to continual threats, which reached its peak in November 2020, when an agent entered the rapper Denis Solís's home without a warrant in order to arrest him. Solís was handcuffed, beaten and incarcerated; within two days, he'd been rushed through a trial and sentenced to eight months in jail.

Solís's fellow Movement members tried to have him liberated from the prison where he was being held, but state security wouldn't let them visit him or protest. Anyone who showed up to support the rapper was detained. The members of the Movement then decided to hold their demonstrations in the street rather than at the prison—but, again, they were prevented from doing so. They eventually ended up at Luis Manuel's house, now officially the main hub of the Movement, where they decided that their only viable tactic was a hunger strike.

The strike lasted a week. One evening, the whole country mysteriously lost internet access, which meant that the public couldn't watch as security agents disguised as doctors broke into Luis Manuel's house and arrested all fourteen of the people there. The agents claimed that they were engaged in a public health measure to stop the spread of the coronavirus. The next morning, hundreds of young people, many of them artists, surrounded the Ministry of Culture, demanding, among other things, freedom for the San Isidro Movement members and a dialogue between state representatives and civil society groups. No such dialogue occurred, but the demonstrations did lead to the creation of a new movement, 27N, that agitates for "the right to have rights."

Another result of the demonstrations was the song "Patria y Vida," which was made by rappers living outside Cuba along with two members of the San Isidro Movement, Maykel Osorbo and El Funky. The song's lyrics subverted Fidel's famous slogan, "Patria o Muerte" (Homeland or Death), to demand the end of dictatorship in Cuba. The song quickly became a hymn of change for the young dissidents, gaining such dramatic popularity that the government banned it from the airwaves.

The Movement also released a music video featuring Luis Manuel, which gained one million views on YouTube within three days. For the regime, this international reaction was the last straw. Within a few months, the majority of the San Isidro Movement's members were in hiding, in exile, or in maximum-security prisons. Afrik3 Reina is one of the few still living freely in Cuba—if you can call her situation freedom.

* * *

Afrik3 Reina was born in Madruga, a town on the eastern border of Mayabeque that has a very strong tradition of Afro-Cuban religion. Her main connection to her faith was her grandmother, who worshipped Obatalá, the Yoruba deity. She brought Afrik3 to the ceremonies she attended, and though Afrik3 was too young to understand, she was still shaped by the songs, prayers and dances she heard and saw.

When Afrik3 was seven, her grandmother died of stomach cancer. Her family held a vigil at home, dressing her grandmother as Obatalá "in a beautiful white suit and crown." At one point, Afrik3 went up to the coffin to kiss her grandmother goodbye. However, after the vigil, Afrik3 says that "things started happening in the night. My brother began letting lose these bloodcurdling screams in his sleep, and I was walking around the house with my eyes closed because I was scared of what I thought I saw."

What Afrik3 thought she saw was a red-eyed black bull with its legs shackled and chained. Afrik3 was so afraid that she tried to avoid her home after dark. When she did go home to sleep, she curled up by her bedroom door because she thought that somebody was hiding under her mattress. She would also hold her pee all night because she was frightened to leave her room. "Two years went by before my parents had a mass in the house," Afrik3 says. "My grandmother's spirit came and told me that I didn't need to be afraid if I felt something on my skin or hair, it was just her. She also said that the bull was part of a hundred-year-old *nganga* we hadn't known was in the house. A *nganga*, in the Palo Monte religion, is a vessel that holds material and spiritual energies. You can put all sorts of things in it, including human or animal bones, and the objects create vibrations related to earth, metal, or fire."

* * *

In high school, Afrik3 befriended a group of classmates who listened to North American hip-hop, dressed like rappers and, twice a month, met at a local gallery that let them use its space to listen to music and try out dances they'd learned from American movies. She heard Cuban rap for the first time through those kids. "My grandmother had wanted me to be an artist," she says, "and I wanted to be a musician like my dad. He was a drummer, not professionally or anything, but he'd play shows and bring me along, even let me go on stage. But after high school, he and my teachers thought I should go to vocational school, not art school like I wanted. On the day of the history test I had to take to get in, there was also a test to get into the art teachers' college (known formally as the Art Teachers Program), and I went to that one instead. I'd never really rebelled before. I went home and told my dad what I'd done, and he was furious."

After shouting at her, her father announced, "Well, you're not going to vocational school, but you're not going to that art school, either." Instead, he made her enroll at a regular university, where she quickly became depressed. She stopped eating, and threw up constantly from hunger. Weight fell off her. Her period stopped. When her father realized what was happening, he let her go to the art teachers' college.

* * *

Founding a school for art teachers was a component of Fidel Castro's "battle of ideas," an early 2000s initiative that included over 200 educational and patriotic programs. Castro intended to sell the world a vision of Cuba as capable of rising above the "menace of the United States government," which meant that many of the programs were designed less to change life in Cuba than to create good data. Castro wanted numbers to sell, numbers to disguise the Cuban reality, numbers to enhance Cuba's image.

In his speeches, Fidel frequently extolled the art teachers' college: its graduation rates, the quality of its students and the speed with which they went from the classroom to communities across the country. But he never mentioned the real reasons many enrolled at the school. According to Afrik3, "a lot of the male students were there not because they loved art, but because it got them out of military service. People also came because they didn't have to study science, and once they graduated, they could go to any humanities school at the University of Havana without taking entrance exams."

Afrik3 studied choral singing and special education at the art teachers' college, and upon graduating, got a job teaching the latter in El Límite, an isolated village on the border of Mayabeque and Matanzas. Her school had forty or so students, ranging in age from five to twenty, "which was very difficult, because the Cuban special-ed curriculum is done by age, not ability. You don't have different classes or programs for children with Down's or autism or severe intellectual disabilities. Everyone gets the same thing. In music class, we had to give them boxes and sticks, since we didn't have instruments. All I got as teaching tools were a cassette player and a thumb drive."

After two years at the school, Afrik3 became the leader of the art teachers' brigade in Mayabeque. Soon, she was going to war with the directors of the province's Union of Communist Youth, who wanted the teachers to provide music and art for the Mayabeque government's events. Afrik3 maintained that art teachers were for teaching art, not politics. Her confrontation with the union cost Afrik3 her job.

* * *

After losing her position in El Límite, Afrik3 recognized that disobedience wasn't a good way to survive in Cuba. At the same time, she also realized that she was able to deal with setbacks, which gave her the strength to do what she'd always dreamed of: living in Havana. She moved to the city, crashing on a cousin's couch, and found a job as a singing coach for a lyric stage company. Soon, she was going out and exploring her new home. Africk3 discovered that after dark, Avenida de los Presidentes, a street in Vedado, turned into a party, full of young people sitting in the grass, drinking and singing and getting high. She had never imagined this Havana, and she wanted to be part of it. Slowly, she made friends in the scene. "I was the hot Black girl with dreads reciting poetry and smoking cigarettes all night," she says. "I wanted to rap, really, but I didn't have any music, just what I could do with rhythm. It was pretty much spoken word, though I had never heard of it."

A member of Afrik3's audience mentioned her performances to Queen Nzinga Maxwell, a Costa Rican spoken word performer and artist who was in Cuba to put on a festival called "Vientre Evolución." The festival was a celebration of International Afro-Descendant Women's Day, and Queen was hoping to attract Black families from all over Cuba. She imagined a program consisting of African instruments, a spoken word album being recorded in real time, a swelling of Afrodiasporic consciousness. She'd recruited the pianist Chucho Valdés and other big-deal Cuban cultural talents, but she was on the hunt for a poet. Once she saw Afrik3 in action, she knew she'd found what she was looking for.

"I didn't know anything about spoken word," Afrik3 remembers, "but Queen said that didn't matter. I was doing it already, whether I knew it or not. She and I rehearsed together a couple times, and she coached me, but in the end, the recording and the festival didn't happen. She'd been a political prisoner in Costa Rica for joining their version of the Black Panthers, and the [Cuban] government got all paranoid about her and shut it down."

Still, the two performers' friendship grew. It was Queen who gave Afrik3 her name. "People were already calling me Africa because of my dreads and the way I dressed—I always wore loose, colorful clothes—and Queen said that on the continent, women name their daughters Africa to give them strength and grounding. We thought it made sense to add 'reina,' but instead of having me be the queen, we reversed it so that Africa is the queen. We added the 3 because it represented spiritual insight in ancient Egypt."

One of Queen's art practices involved painting with menstrual blood, which Afrik3 Reina also took up. "It helped me get closer to both my femininity and my African heritage," she says. "In ancestral Africa, women would go to communal huts to bleed, and when a girl got her period, it was a whole religious celebration. Our periods were divine instruments. It was colonialism that made us dislike them."

* * *

As Afrik3 settled into her new life as an artist in Havana, she began to see a phenomenon that had not been present in her hometown, dominated as it was by the Afro-Cuban tradition: racism. Cops constantly demanded her Black friends' papers in the street. They never asked Afrik3, though, as her clothes made people think she wasn't Cuban. (At bars and clubs, hustlers hunting foreign women tried to pick her up.)

Increasingly, Afrik3 was compelled to take a stand. She needed to do more about anti-Blackness than write a poem or a song. So she founded an arts organization called Puentes del Sol in Cayo Hueso, a poor, majority-Black part of Central Havana, to teach primary-school students dance, creative writing and spoken word. Her goal was to help the kids play with language and with their bodies. Nearly all the students who came to her were Black children who ordinarily used their free time to prowl the Callejón de Hamel, an Afrocentric tourist site, asking foreigners for money. She wanted to give the kids the artistic tools to help them change their situations, to emancipate themselves through spoken word. "In Cuba, Black people are afraid of speaking out or struggling for a cause," Afrika3 says. "We're afraid not only of what we could lose now, but what's already been taken from us historically. We're used to the Revolution saying it saved us, it's the only reason we're still in Cuba, and so we should shut up and be grateful rather than demanding to be taken seriously as part of the country and culture. It's just more colonial thought."

* * *

In April 2021, Luis Manuel decided to hold a birthday party for a boy in San Isidro whom he had grown close to. The child's father wasn't around, and his mother struggled to support the boy and her three other children. Luis Manuel also wanted to use the boy's birthday as an excuse to throw a party for all the neighborhood children, many of whom didn't have access to books, toys, art supplies or even candy. His idea was that the Movement could give those things out as presents.

When they found out about the party, however, state security claimed that it was an effort by "mercenary artists" to corrupt Pioneers' Day, the annual celebration of the country's youth organizations. In social media posts, state security said that the toys, candy and other gifts that the Movement promised to give the neighborhood children had been bought with money from North American organizations trying to "defeat the Revolution." State security then decided to throw its own party in San Isidro to "show its concern for the residents." Luis Manuel tried to livestream the event on Facebook, but a swarm of state security agents dragged him away in handcuffs. He ended up in a prison cell for the rest of the day.

Afrik3 Reina, who'd been heading to San Isidro when Luis Manuel got arrested, resumed the livestream when she arrived. In her posts, you can see neighborhood children and their parents in the doorways of their homes, watching complete strangers—the children of state security agents—eat and play in the street.

On the day of the Movement's party, the streets around Luis Manuel's home looked like a war zone. Plainclothes agents turned children away from his house. Luis Manuel and a clown he'd hired for the party then emerged with sacks of books and candy, hoping to throw them over the police barrier to the children, but the agents tackled and arrested them. After they were taken away, the Movement decided to smuggle the gifts to the children in the neighborhood, but state security reacted by going house to house, confiscating the "mercenary" toys, candy, and books.

From then on, state security maintained an occupying presence in San Isidro. The excuse was that the Eighth Congress of the Cuban Communist Party (CCP)—the country's one legal political party—was soon going to be held nearby. (This turned out to be the congress where Miguel Díaz-Canel took over from Raúl Castro, a succession in name only: Díaz-Canel said, in his first speech as secretary of the CCP, that he would consult Castro on all major strategic decisions.)

Luis Manuel's house was under siege for twenty-two days. Nobody visited him but Afrik3 Reina. "I went every day," she says. "He was exhausted and broken. He tried channeling his feelings into art, but eventually he couldn't stand it. That was when he told me it was time for the Garrote Vil."

The "Garrote Vil" was a work of performance art that Luis Manuel had been planning for a long time. It would consist of him sitting in his house for eight hours a day in a strangulation device called a garrote vil. He would remain in the device for five days—during the time that the CCP congress took place—daring the government to deliver its judgment and execute him. As further enticement, he'd leave the door of his house open.

"After the first day of the performance," Afrik3 recalls, "we put on music to relax. Right away, the agents surrounding the house started blasting political songs from a loudspeaker on the corner. Luis Manuel went into the street and started to dance. After he came back inside, two agents followed him, acting all friendly, wanting to know if his performance was done until tomorrow. We said yes, and they left. I started cooking, but Luis Manuel watched them from the door. He could tell something was going to happen. All of a sudden he ran for his phone, and I knew they were coming for us."

It took seven agents to pin Luis Manuel to the floor. They cuffed his hands behind his back and beat him. Two women and a man wrestled Afrik3 Reina's phone from her hands, spraining her wrist and finger in the process, as she attempted to record the scene. Both Luis Manuel and Afrik3 were taken from the house in handcuffs, barefoot and without masks. Outside, the agents put them in separate patrol cars, yelling as loudly as they could, "¡Viva la Revolución! ¡Viva Fidel! ¡Patria o muerte!" In the kitchen, Afrik3's chicken stew was still simmering on the stove.

Afrik3 wound up at the Cerro police station. Still unmasked at the height of the pandemic, she sat alone in a dark room. Eventually a cop turned the light on, greeted her, and sat a few meters away, leafing through a notebook. On the walls hung paintings of the Castro brothers and the rest of the country's military leadership. More police officers came in, some greeting her as if they knew her, others glaring at her for not wearing a mask. When the chief entered, he told her to leave the room, as a meeting was about to start. "I sat alone in a hallway for hours," Afrik3 remembers. "After a while, they took me to an interrogation room with two cameras and a microphone. They brought my phone and asked me to give them the passcode, but I wouldn't, so they started threatening to take away my son. At the end of the interrogation, they took me home—in a car with a motorcycle escort, like I was Bin Laden—and put me under house arrest. For eight days, I had agents under my balcony around the clock."

Luis Manuel had been freed as well, but the art he'd made during the siege was gone from his house, and his kitchen was charred from the stew catching fire. He wanted to protest to get his work back, but every time he left his house, he was arrested. For a week, it was a cycle: he left his house, was detained for a day, then came home. After that, he decided it was time for a new hunger strike, which lasted seven days before state security took him to a hospital by force. He remained there, imprisoned and incommunicado, for a month.

* * *

"I cry every time I have to move," Afrik3 shares. "When it happens, my son runs his hand over my face and smiles at me. He always waves goodbye to our houses and our neighbors cheerfully, like everything's okay. It's like he's trying to tell me, 'Our home is us, not this place,' but he's three and he still isn't talking, and I know it's because of everything we've gone through."

In July 2021, Cuba saw its biggest anti-government uprising in six decades. In towns across the country, thousands of citizens took to the streets, demanding an end to the dictatorship. Over 1400 people were arrested, among them Luis Manuel. Before the uprising, the rapper Maykel Osorbo was arrested while eating lunch in his house. Both are in maximum-security prisons.

As she waits for the money her friends raised for her, Afrik3 has been trying to get the incarcerated members of the San Isidro Movement out of jail. Recently, she has been making videos artworks where she sings to her Yoruba deities, asking for mercy for Cuba. Her works are at once prayers for political prisoners and calls for compassion and peace among Cubans. The series is titled "Manos de Bruja." Describing one of the videos, Afrik3 says, "You can't slow down magic, you can't cover light, you can't tie up language, and you can't stop the universe from siding with justice and prosperity."

NAMIBIA FLORES'S IMPOSSIBLE FIGHT

Namibia Flores's life has always been a battle against her own reflection. But no matter what she does, she can't beat it. At the age of forty-five, she throws punches at herself in the mirror of the living room of the house she rents in Miramar, her arms shooting forward as if on springs. Her movements possess an ephemeral grace, an elegance that does not conceal the deadliness of her blows. If she hit you, you'd fall straight to the ground.

The mirror is located just outside the kitchen, in a room with no furniture. It's where Namibia goes to expel stress, grief and regret. In her imagination, the bare room is a ring surrounded by red and blue ropes.

She glares at her image as if it were the enemy. She moves her feet in a syncopated dance, feinting and weaving, trying to trick herself as she releases a combination of left fist, right fist, left, right, as if she could punch her face out of the mirror. But no matter how hard she swings, her nemesis remains before her.

Her body is practically a marble statue. She's Black, five foot two, with more than thirty tattoos curving taut over her muscles. Although she no longer trains daily, she's still a contained mass of strength, a true physical marvel.

Namibia has never been knocked out in a fight. She's never lost on points. Namibia Flores has actually never fought in a real match because in Cuba, which has won forty-one Olympic gold medals in boxing and over eighty more in world championships, women are forbidden to box competitively.

For years, Namibia trained day and night, waiting and hoping for a change in government policy. Her dream was to box for her country—a dream she would have achieved if she were a man, and that, in nearly any other country on earth, she would have had the right to pursue. But she was up against not only the regime, but time, which ultimately defeated her in the end: Cuban boxing is governed by the rules of the International Boxing Federation, which says that boxers must stop competing at the age of forty.

* * *

Many women in Cuba box in gyms, in public plazas, and at home, but the vast majority do it as a means, not an end. For them, boxing is a workout, a way to sweat, to lose weight or avoid gaining it, to blow off steam. What else could it be, when boxing is the only sport on the island from which women are banned?

Cuba has one living professional female boxer. She's 102. Her name is Felicia Mesa, and she lives in Sagua la Grande, in Villa Clara. She fought fifteen matches in the 1950s, before Fidel Castro came to power and banned professional boxing. Castro saw anything that smelled of markets or business or money as a threat, and so Felicia, like every other professional athlete on the island, had her career cut short. Many left Cuba to chase their dreams; others chose amateurism at home. Felicia turned to agriculture.

In Cuba today, amateur athletic competition is a regime within the regime. No Cuban athlete may join a league outside the country; if they sign a contract abroad, their right to compete for Cuba is revoked. It's as if the midfielder Héctor Herrera forfeited his position on Mexico's national team when he signed his contract with Atlético de Madrid.

Cuban athletes' salaries are set according to the state system. The country's athletic elite, its Olympians, earn a base monthly salary of 5590 pesos, or $80. Medalists can earn extra money: a gold is worth $35, a silver $23, and a bronze $17. In a month, then, a Cuban gold medal winner can earn enough to eat badly and dress poorly. If women's boxing were legal, Namibia, as a member of the national team, would have earned far less: 3725 pesos, or $53.

Some of the leading figures in Cuban boxing have made their thoughts on women competing well-known. In 2013, Alberto Puig, President of the Cuban Boxing Federation, said, "We're uneasy with the image of a woman in gloves. We don't see a place for them in the sport. But we're carrying out medical and psychological research on the suitability of boxing for women, and we reserve the right to change our minds." His predecessor, José Barrientos, didn't hedge his bets. When he was in charge of the Federation, he said flatly, "We aren't interested in international women's boxing. We don't think it's appropriate." In 2009, the decorated coach Pedro Roque announced that, "Cuban women are there to show their beautiful faces, not take punches." Three years later, he coached USA Women's Boxing at the Olympics. Evidently, leaving Cuba changed his attitude, as ditching his macho ideas gave him the chance to coach Claressa Shields, the middleweight gold medalist at women's boxing's inaugural Olympics. Shields made Roque part of women's boxing history.

Such sexist ideas are hardly new, nor are female boxers struggling against them. In the 1720s, when neither gloves nor rules had been invented, the English boxer Elizabeth Wilkinson overcame misogyny to fight. In 1876, Nell Saunders and Rose

Harland fought the first women's boxing match in the United States. Fast forwarding one hundred years, the 1970s saw a wave of women petitioning their states to give them licenses to box. However, every application was denied except those of Cathy Davis, Jackie Tonawanda and Marian Trimiar, who successfully sued the state of New York. But although the trial generated widespread public sympathy, the plaintiffs' victory didn't help other women boxers. By 1987, discrimination against female boxers remained extreme enough that Trimiar launched a hunger strike in the hopes of earning parity in the sport.

In 1992, Gail Grandchamp won the right to box in a suit against the state of Massachusetts. Her victory was hollow, though: her suit had lasted eight years, and by the time it was over, she was over the age of thirty-six, the sport's age cut-off. But a year later, Dallas Malloy, at sixteen, successfully sued USA Boxing to accept women across the country. This opened the door to the 1996 match, fought in the United States, that is now considered the start of professional women's boxing: Christy Martin (USA) vs. Deidre Gogarty (Ireland). The same year, the United Kingdom lifted its 116-year-old ban on the sport, and gradually, nations around the world followed suit, leading to the creation of the Women's International Boxing Association.

* * *

Namibia Flores claims that she's the same age as the sovereign nation of Namibia, but she's not. She was born on February 15th, 1976, while Namibia, the nation, didn't achieve independence from apartheid South Africa until 1990. In 1975, though, Cuba sent troops to aid in some African freedom fights, and the obstetrician and nurses who delivered her suggested the name Namibia, which they'd been hearing constantly on the news, to her parents, who'd shown up at the hospital in Matanzas without a clue what to call their baby girl.

Namibia has some two million inhabitants spread over 318,772 square miles. It's highly arid, the driest country in sub-Saharan Africa, but its immense desert sustains a tremendous variety of fauna. Namibia's animals overcome the desolation of the desert—its rough sand, its scarce water—just as Namibia Flores has had to overcome years of violence and abuse.

Dysfunction was part of Namibia's life from the start. Although she's her parents' second child, their relationship was always long-distance, since her mother's parents disapproved of her father, who was white and a convicted criminal. In 1980, he left Cuba as part of the Mariel boatlift, a mass emigration which Castro agreed to after a political crisis initiated by a group of citizens who hijacked a bus and crashed in into the Peruvian Embassy in order to demand asylum. Part of his consent was the stipulation that all "stains on society" emigrate. Namibia didn't see her father again until 1999.

Namibia describes her childhood as "hectic and traumatic." She attended eleven primary schools, mainly in Matanzas and Havana, because her mother was constantly moving in with new men. Namibia and her sister were always dragged along, as was her younger half-brother, who was born while their mother was renting a crumbling room in Las Margaritas, a Havana tenement that was once home to Celia Cruz. The boy's father died there after accidentally drinking a bottle of grain alcohol, thinking it was rum.

Namibia remembers life in Las Margaritas as essentially living outdoors, since their roof let in the rain. She and her siblings would chew wax and pretend it was gum. "We were like the children you see staring into store windows," she says.

Their mother would frequently lock her children in the apartment and go out partying. While she was dancing and drinking, Namibia and her siblings would fight over the tin can of sugar water their mother had left them for dinner. Namibia has a scar on her face from the time her sister Mabel hit her with the can. Mabel, who was seven then, was in charge of Namibia, three, and their brother Gilberto, two. "My mother has an intellectual disability," explains Namibia. "She failed first grade, and she never learned to read or write. I'm sure she wouldn't have made those decisions otherwise."

Namibia's mother eventually gave up the place in Las Margaritas to move to Cárdenas, in Matanzas, with a man. She only brought Mabel along with her. Namibia and Gilberto moved in with their grandmother in Havana's Luyanó neighborhood. There, the children's lives grew even worse. "My grandmother still had all her grown sons at home," Namibia remembers. "One of them was a nurse, one was in and out of prison, one was a mechanic, one was in the army, and one was a bum. She had two bedrooms and slept in one by herself. In the other room, it was me and my brother in one bed, an uncle in another, and a second uncle on the floor. We had mats in the living room and dining room where the other three slept."

In the mornings, the house was a mess: sheets on the ground, pillows everywhere. Namibia and Gilberto were in charge of tidying up. After putting the bedding away, they had to clean the rest of the house, take the trash out, and do the previous day's dishes. Namibia recalls, "My grandmother always said, 'If you want to watch cartoons in the afternoon, you'd better do all your chores in the morning.'"

* * *

It was a year and a half before their mother returned. On hearing how her children were living, she decided to take them to Cárdenas, but three months later, she and her boyfriend broke up and the family returned to Luyanó—a move that happened several more times, finally ending when Namibia was in fifth grade.

Of all the moves, the last one was by far the most traumatic. Namibia's mother had taken up with a man who lived in Oriente, which was so far east that she couldn't afford to take herself and her children there. In order to pursue the romance, she left her kids with a distant relative named Maritza, who lived in Cárdenas and had done time in prison for belonging to an infamous violent gang called Los 46, known for beating mugging victims to death. When Namibia and her siblings arrived at Maritza's house, clinging to their mother's hands, they heard shouts through the half-open door. Nobody answered their knocks, so they let themselves in, where they saw Maritza chasing furiously after her shrieking, terrified son, throwing objects at him.

For the next two months, the children's life was a nightmare. Maritza hit them if they took too long when she sent them out to buy bread, or talked too loudly, or played indoors. She delighted in punishing the children, and was endlessly ingenious in making them suffer. "She'd have us kneel on rice or bottle caps while holding bricks straight out from our chests," Namibia remembers, "or leave us on the patio for hours when the sun was hot enough to melt rock."

One day Maritza served the four children a meal, telling them that each one could have three pieces of pork. She left the room and, upon returning, saw that someone had exceeded their allotment. One by one, she marched the kids to the kitchen and made them drink saltwater until they vomited so that she could see who had disobeyed her.

Shortly after, Mabel got gastroenteritis and had to be hospitalized. When she was released, she told the doctors that Maritza, who'd come to get her, was a stranger, and that she had no family. Maritza stormed home to collect Namibia and dragged her to the hospital as proof of her relationship with Mabel and her siblings. But while Maritza was gone, Mabel had made up her mind to escape. When she saw them coming, she waved at Namibia, jumped out the nearest window, and ran. After that, she lived in one of the province's orphanages.

On hearing this story, the children's grandmother came to Cárdenas. Namibia and Gilberto begged her to take them with her. "Our choices were cleaning a house in Havana or waiting to be beaten to death in Cárdenas," Namibia says.

* * *

Returning to Luyanó led to Namibia's introduction to sports. Her new school had a basketball team, and the gym teacher, after seeing her explosive speed, recruited Namibia to join. The practices became the highlight of Namibia's day. As she dribbled and shot, she realized that she could escape her life. "School and basketball were my refuge," she says. "I got some peace there. I didn't have to worry about home."

At home, things were essentially the same as they had been the first time she lived with her grandmother: Namibia and her brother cleaned and scrubbed, while their uncles did nothing. Only one thing had changed: their grandmother now sold bread and soda in the living room in the afternoons. During that time, she would shut her grandchildren away in the bedroom so that they wouldn't get in the way. The "bum" uncle would grab a drink and a slice of bread, go into the bedroom, and make his niece and nephew fight for the food. He'd laugh, watching them kick and hit each other until the loser could no longer stand.

When the army uncle learned about this—and learned that Namibia always lost—he decided to coach her to defend herself. He was the one who brought martial arts into her life. Her uncle would raise his hand and yell "kick." Namibia would then swing one leg higher than her ribs to reach his palm, and he'd strike the other, sending her straight to the ground. As she lay in a heap, he'd shout, "Up! Up! Let's go!" and up she'd get, though soon she'd be back down again. Slowly, she grew stronger. She'd tell her uncle she hated training and wanted to quit, but he'd insist, "No, no, you like it," and eventually, when he hit her support leg, she didn't go down.

Years later, Namibia would dedicate her life to combat sports. But at the time, all she wanted was to play, have fun, and get away from her poisonous home environment, which seemed impossible. "My brother and I would play catch in the alley," she recalls, "but we had a neighbor who got annoyed with us and complained to my army uncle. He beat us with his belt, and once he was done, my grandmother did it again."

On ten separate occasions, Namibia and Gilberto decided to run away to the orphanage, convinced that Mabel had to be living a better life then they were. They would leave the house, walk through the alley where they played catch, jump a wall, and take a bus to the port, where they would ride the ferry connecting Old Havana to Casablancas. When they got there, they would catch a train to Matanzas—sneaking on every form of transportation, since they had no money.

They only reached the orphanage twice and only got to speak to Mabel once. "We always got caught by the cops," Namibia says, "and of course they asked what we were doing traveling such a long way with no documents and no adult. We'd have to tell them our address, and then they'd take us back to our grandmother, who'd have us cleaning the house within minutes of getting home. She'd wait for us to miss a spot, and then hit us with the broom until it broke and then throw water on the floor for us to start mopping again."

* * *

When Namibia was in seventh grade, her mother came back. She got out of an old American car, completely toothless, curlers on her head, and said, "I came to get you." They all drove to get Mabel at the orphanage and, from there, to Manzanillo, where their mother had been living since she left her children with Maritza.

All three siblings were astounded by Eastern Cuba. They'd barely seen the beach in Havana, and now it was down the street. For a month, they pretended to go to school, but went swimming all day instead. When their mother caught on, she sent Gilberto, the ringleader, back to Havana, hoping his sisters would behave without his bad influence. Instead, Namibia missed him so much that she decided to return to Havana, too. Without saying goodbye to her mother, she hitchhiked across the island, riding with trucker after trucker, without a cent to pay her way.

Upon arriving in Luyanó, Namibia learned that her brother had been sent to reform school. Sports became her distraction from the pain of being so far from him. "I made the municipal basketball team," she says, "but I could only practice if I got away from my grandmother. She liked to say cleaning was my sport. I never played in a single game. I was always doing dishes or washing clothes or scrubbing floors."

Missing games was hard on Namibia, but not nearly as hard as her *quinceañera*, which is a celebration of a girl's fifteenth birthday, marking her passage into womanhood. "My grandmother insisted on throwing a big party and putting me in a huge dress with heels and a shitload of makeup," Namibia recalls. "I hated it. I was a tomboy. I didn't want to wear any of that. And besides, the party was just a reason for my family to get drunk. My grandmother had it at her friend's house and only let me invite three friends. Mostly it was adults who'd kicked in for the party. My grandmother and uncles spent all the money on getting drunk."

By then Mabel had had a baby, and Namibia and Gilberto, who'd come home, decided to travel to Oriente to see her. Soon after arriving, the two of them joined a dominoes game in the neighborhood. Whoever lost had to chug a glass of water as a penalty. Without anybody noticing, Gilberto snuck hot pepper into the glass. "I thought those hicks would murder us," Namibia remembers. "My brother had to hide for a week, and when he came out, one of the neighbor boys still wanted to beat him up. I got in the middle and said that I was older, and that if he wanted to hit someone, he could hit me."

An adult saw what was happening and separated the two teenagers. He told Namibia that if she was going to be that courageous, she'd better learn self-defense, and suggested she attend taekwondo classes at a nearby sports club. Training there reminded Namibia of her uncle's martial arts lessons. Within three months, she'd beaten every girl in her weight class and been recruited to the province's Escuelas de Iniciación Deportiva Escolar, which are high schools for children who show promise in sports.

Initially, Namibia trained all week at school and went home on the weekends, but returning to that house was torture. "A lot of times there wasn't food," she says, "and my mom and stepdad would kick me out, anyway. I'd go over to my sister's. She had a second baby by then. The house belonged to her husband's family, and I could sleep in their cobwebby basement. One time the husband came down to the basement and tried to rape me, but I pretended to be asleep. I closed my eyes and ignored him, and maybe that's why he didn't do anything in the end. I don't even know if he jerked off."

After that, Namibia decided to live at school until graduation. However, that came with its own set of problems. When her classmates were gone on the weekends, the janitorial staff would break into their rooms to steal things, which Namibia got blamed for. She eventually saw no choice but to return to Havana, even though it put her taekwondo career at risk: leaving the athletic high school system meant she couldn't get recruited to the national team.

* * *

Namibia spent the next two years selling candy before she began teaching youth taekwondo at a sports center in Santos Suárez, near the tenements of her childhood. She had such good results that the city gave her a job training high schoolers in San Isidro and the opportunity to take night school classes in physical education.

Her new workplace was next door to the famous Rafael Trejo boxing gym, which has trained more Cuban champions than anywhere in the world. Before she went to her night classes, Namibia would stand in the gym, watching boys and men of all ages dance in the ring as their gloves whipped through the air.

One day she asked a coach if she could hit the heavy bag. He gave her a skeptical look. "Sure, if you use your fists," he told her. "No feet." His name was Naldo Mestre, and before long, he'd be her trainer.

From then on, Namibia trained at Rafael Trejo. She'd learn boxing stances and techniques, then tug her white dobok over her shorts and shirt and go teach her taekwondo classes. However, the principal of the school wasn't happy with her. She said that Namibia's students would imitate her if they saw her in the boxing gym, and that it wasn't appropriate for a woman to box. The principal gave Namibia an ultimatum: quit Rafael Trejo or lose her job. Namibia hung up her dobok and kept her gloves on.

* * *

It was 2006, and after three months of working out in the gym, Namibia still hadn't fought anyone. That was when a female Dutch boxer turned up at Rafael Trejo to train. She was huge and blonde, and had boxed professionally in Europe for a decade. Naldo Mestre asked Namibia, "Ready to challenge her?"

"You know I am," Namibia answered.

During the match, Namibia went at the Dutch woman like an animal. Her training was working; she could do what she'd learned against an international pro. She hit and hit, crashing toward the other boxer like a train. But after several rounds, Namibia's opponent got her on the ropes. As she jabbed and uppercut, it became evident that she'd been using the earlier rounds as a warmup. Before long, Mestre called the fight.

"Amazing," the Dutch woman murmured as she left the ring. Neither Namibia nor Mestre spoke English, and not until later did Namibia realize what her opponent had meant, and that it wasn't an insult, but praise for her abilities.

* * *

A few years later, Wu Ching-Kuo, then head of the International Boxing Association, visited Cuba, with an agenda that included gaining approval for women's boxing on the island. Confident that Wu would succeed, Mestre called Namibia and told her that he would coach her exclusively from then on.

However, she still had a ways to go before she was ready for real competition. She had to learn to never close her eyes, always maintain her guard, and move her back leg like a boxer rather than a taekwondo fighter. She also had to start sparring with men, as Cuba didn't have a single woman she could practice with. "It was rough, going up against men," Namibia remembers. "I was always sure I'd cracked a rib by the end." Once, a group of Chinese tourists came to the gym while she was sparring. "All of them started watching me, since I was the only woman," Namibia says. "My opponent got pissed. He wanted attention. He got me in a corner and really started pounding, and without even thinking about it, I turned and kicked him in the face to get him away from me." In the stands, the tourists clapped so hard she thought their hands would fall off.

* * *

In the lead-up to the 2012 Olympics in London, the International Olympic Committee added women's boxing to the games, nearly a century after introducing the men's sport. Unfortunately, Wu's visit hadn't earned Cuban women the right to box. Mestre told Namibia not to lose hope, to concentrate on the Rio Olympics in 2016, though there was no guarantee that the state would cave by then. "Even though the government won't let us box, it's happy to let the women we'd be fighting come here," Namibia points out. She's seen squads of female boxers parade through Rafael Trejo, eager to learn from its celebrated trainers.

Among those teams was the five woman Indonesian squad, who Mestre had Namibia fight. "On the day they arrived," she says, "he put me up against all of them, one by one. I went ten rounds with no break. Those girls wiped the floor with me." Impressed, the Indonesian coach offered to include Namibia in team practices, and one of the boxers invited her to their hotel. Namibia spent a month and a half with the Indonesian team. "I only went to my house to get clothes," she tells me. "I'd get up at 5:00 to run on the coast, and after that, we just trained. I got hit so much my eye was bruised for two weeks. I couldn't go to the dining room, since the Cubans working there would've caught me, so the girls would smuggle me food. When they left, they said I couldn't quit. None of them had seen a boxer like me."

* * *

After the Indonesian visit, Namibia found another woman to box with at the gym. Her name was Meg Smaker, and she was an American who'd come to Cuba to perfect her boxing technique, though she wasn't a pro: she was earning an MFA in documentary filmmaking at Stanford. She and Namibia became friends, and when Meg's time on the island ended, she asked Namibia if she would be the subject of her thesis. Meg thought that the story of a woman who dreamed of boxing for Cuba even though the government banned it would make for a compelling story.

Namibia said yes, and Meg made a fifteen-minute movie. Months later, Namibia got an email from the South by Southwest festival, inviting her to attend as the star of the film, which had been nominated for Best Documentary Short. "I'd never left Cuba," she says. "Meg's friend put us up in Austin. Meg got a bed and I got an air mattress. She told me not to talk to journalists, or anyone but her and her assistant. After a couple of days we switched to a different house, one in the suburbs, and Meg left me there all day. She'd come home drunk from the festival at night. I was alone with no cell phone, no landline, a TV and coffee pot I couldn't work, and had no food but these giant bananas. For a while I thought they were fake, as lots of people in Cuba have fake bananas for décor. I'd left my toothbrush in Cuba, but I never had a chance to tell Meg I needed one. She only came back to the house to sleep."

After four days, Meg's parents arrived and were appalled at what was going on. They took Namibia to get food, a phone, a toothbrush and a coat. A few days later, Namibia went for a run and, she says, "I was so agitated that I just ran and ran and ran. At some point I looked around and it hit me that I had no idea where I was. Eventually I recognized some houses and a towel I'd run by on the sidewalk, and found my way back."

When she arrived, the Smakers were waiting. None of them had mentioned to Namibia that the award presentations were that day. Meg shouted at Namibia to get dressed, and to not bother to shower, as she only had a short time to get ready. So, Namibia went to the ceremony covered in sweat. An hour later, *Boxeadora*, Meg's story of Namibia's life, won Best Documentary Short.

Namibia left the theater and sat alone in the stairwell, leaning her head on the railing. All over the lobby were posters with her face on them. When she returned to the theater, Meg was talking to a group of people that included USA Boxing's women's coach, who invited Namibia to box for the United

States in Rio. Namibia said no. “In that moment, all I wanted was to represent Cuba.”

In the morning, Namibia received a message from a friend in Miami. She said that Namibia’s name was on the news as a “Cuban boxer who’s going to join the U.S. team.” “I started throwing things all over the house,” Namibia remembers. “My friend said that Meg was talking so much shit about the Cuban government that she could get me banned from the country. I thought I’d never see my family again. I was furious. I told Meg she had to buy me a ticket home that second.” Within hours, Namibia was back at Rafael Trejo.

* * *

When Namibia returned from Austin, Mestre told her that her moment had arrived. A cohort of female boxers was now training at the national team’s facility. Although the female boxing ban remained in place, rumors were spreading that a national women’s boxing team was being formed.

As a result, many female athletes from other sports began switching to boxing. Some came from combat sports such as karate, judo, taekwondo and wrestling, but runners, fencers and even volleyball players now wanted to box as well. For example, Yoana Rodríguez, who held Cuba’s under-eighteen world record for the discus, decided to turn to boxing. “I quit discus the day I heard they were going to let us box,” she says. “Boxing was always my dream. My father was a boxer, and he taught me and my brothers when we were tiny. In my house, it was boxing, boxing and more boxing.”

But it was far from smooth sailing for Yoana and her new colleagues. “Some coaches wouldn’t train us,” Yoana shares. “All of them were used to going in and out of the locker rooms, and suddenly we were in there in our bras. When we worked out, people would stick their heads in the gym and go, 'She looks like a man.' It shamed some girls into quitting. I remember one of my teammates was still in high school, and her parents had no idea she was boxing. She'd show up in her uniform and change at the gym. But then some man told her she was too young and hot to get her nose smashed, and we never saw her again."

Legnis Cala, a long and triple jumper, was on maternity leave when she heard the rumors about women's boxing becoming legal. She switched to the sport because, she says, "I thought it would be fun to try something new. But it didn't last. In the end, the government didn't lift the ban, and so we had to give up."

Idamelys Moreno, a 100-and 200-meter sprinter who also switched to boxing, says, "Women's wrestling and weightlifting went through this, too. If the government let women do those sports, at some point they'll let us box, too. I just don't know when."

Eventually, it came out that the Cuban Boxing Federation had never formally said that women could train for Rio. Thus, many of the women who had been excited to box at the Olympic games abandoned their gloves. Others, however, retained hope. Yoana Rodríguez says, "My daughter is seven, and she wants to go where her mother couldn't. I hope when she grows up her dream of boxing can come true."

* * *

Asked why the Cuban government won't let women box, Ailynn Torres, a Cuban postdoctoral researcher at the Latin American Faculty of Social Sciences in Ecuador, says the explanation is institutionalized patriarchy. Cuban society isn't just macho in a cultural sense, she explains, "but in the sense that our lives are arranged around gender inequality. Men have more access to the economy, to the public sphere, to positions of power." But as a feminist, Torres sees hope in "women's increasingly visible fight for our rights. Besides, the president has begun talking about instances of sex discrimination, which suggests that there's some comprehension of the subject, even if he sees them as isolated incidents rather than interconnected ones."

Alcides Sagarra, now eighty-five, is an icon of Cuban boxing. In his time, he trained the two greatest fighters of the past fifty years, Teófilo Stevenson and Félix Savón, both three-time Olympic gold medalists. He also coached 30 other gold medalists, 63 world champions, and 64 junior world champions. He says of women's boxing, "It's happening all over the world. I don't understand why it's still illegal in Cuba. It's ridiculous. Women are soldiers, security guards, drivers. Why shouldn't they box? We coaches have lost time, medals, and the satisfaction of training them. I hope I live to see them in the ring."

Rolando Acebal, the principal trainer of the men's national team, is one of the few other men who have called for women to be allowed to fight. "We have to wait for the Federation to do its analysis," he told me, "but they have to let women box. It's a right. Anyone who can get behind the wheel of a tractor or a plane—anyone who can shoot a gun—can box. Why deny women their opportunity to train and compete? You see mothers protesting for their daughters' right to do it. And you know, in all the years the Federation spends on its studies, we just fall further and further behind."

* * *

Anyone else would have sunken into disappointment, bitterness and frustration. But Namibia, on the ropes since childhood, wasn't about to give in. Even after she turned forty, she kept training. "I'm stubborn," she says. "If I can't get in here, I go over there. My grandmother didn't want me to play basketball, so I played catch until I got beaten. Sports are my thing. I need them. Boxing is what gives me life, and I'm not giving it up until I don't have any choice at all."

At her age, Namibia can only succeed outside of Cuba. Some Chilean friends from her time at university recently put her in touch with two men, also Chilean, who were making a reality show about female boxers in the United States. She traveled to Miami to meet them, not knowing that their real goal wasn't to make a show, but to become her agents and get rich. But on her arrival, they were shocked to learn that she'd never fought a single professional round.

In the United States, no professional will get in the ring with an unknown adversary. Losing to an unranked boxer would hurt their ranking, and so Namibia's would-be agents decided to get her some opponents in the Dominican Republic. While they worked on that, they sent her to a Cuban immigrant's gym to train. But in the end, their plan was a $40,000 failure, and they sent Namibia back to Cuba.

Before going home, Namibia decided to look for her father. She knew he lived in Miami and sometimes played dominoes on Calle Ocho. She hadn't seen him since his visit to Cuba in 1999, when, she remembers, "We spent twenty-one days together. We slept in the same room. I was hugging him constantly. But after he left, I never heard from him again. He disappeared. I thought I might as well see if I could find him while I was in his city, but locating one person in the United States is like finding a needle in a haystack. I walked the whole length of Calle Ocho twice. I thought maybe my dad would be a source of the love I never had, but I didn't have any luck."

* * *

Not long after Namibia's trip to the United States, Maceo Frost, a Swedish director, reached out to her. He ended up making a documentary about her called *Too Beautiful: Our Right to Fight*. The film ends with Namibia en route to Europe to try and box after striking out in the U.S., but once again, she discovers that nobody will risk a match with an unranked fighter. It was beginning to seem that the universe was against her, that she'd reached the age at which one accepts one's destiny rather than trying to change it.

But in that moment, a new opportunity appeared. A mixed martial arts trainer sent Namibia a Facebook message, saying he'd heard her story and that her only option was UFC. "I can help you get into it," he said. UFC, or Ultimate Fighting Championship, is the world's largest mixed martial arts association. Namibia let the trainer bring her to Miami, where she hoped to measure herself against real competition at last.

But the trainer in Miami wanted Namibia to compete at 114 pounds, and she weighed 134. "It's not safe to lose that much that quickly," she explains, "especially in a sport as aggressive as MMA (Mixed Martial Arts.) I wasn't taking that risk."

Instead, she took a break. She didn't see any future options, just an endless line of obstacles. While she dealt with her disappointment, she decided to stay in the United States.

She got a job as a night nurse in Texas, but after a month, she moved to Las Vegas to live with a woman she'd started a relationship with online. But her new girlfriend was extremely jealous and wouldn't let Namibia go out alone or communicate with her friends and family. When Namibia went to the gym, the woman would appear without warning to check on her. One time, during an argument, the woman slammed her own head into the wall, then called the cops to report that she'd been abused. "I was in jail for thirty-six hours," Namibia tells me. "I had to hire a lawyer. He got me out, but the judge made me go to 28 domestic violence classes, do 45 hours of community service and pay $300, and gave me a yearlong restraining order."

Namibia lived by herself after that. She got a job at a casino full of undocumented Cuban staff, working from 2:00 a.m. to 8:30 a.m. She washed, cleaned and sorted cans from the trash, keeping herself awake with drugs. "I was getting high at breakfast and lunch, at work, all day," she says.

One day at home, she looked at herself in the mirror. "This," she told her image, "is not the Namibia I know."

* * *

"I went home and locked myself up in my sister's house in the country," Namibia says. "My niece would come in, see me in my own world, and say, 'Are you okay?' It was my detox after all those drugs."

It was also the end of her career as an athlete. She'd had a meteoric rise from the province where she was born, but now she was back in Matanzas, and there was a global pandemic. While she was there, she learned that her father had died of the coronavirus in Miami. She can't express the strange emotions his death brought up within her: How can one feel the loss of a person you never knew in the first place?

Her greatest grief, however, was that she had never fought a professional fight. She had worked as hard as a person could, and yet she had been defeated without being able to show what she could do. Maybe in Havana, she thought, she'd feel closer to herself.

On returning to the city, she visited her grandmother, now eighty-four and living in Luyanó with just one of Namibia's uncles. Life in the house remained chaotic, and though Namibia had meant to help her grandmother for a few weeks, she found it impossible to stay even that long. Some situations never change, she realized, and she didn't want to let her past drag her down. Instead she turned to the thing she loved. Boxing had made her suffer, but it was still the best way for her to make peace with herself.

Damián Ramos, one of her old sparring partners from Rafael Trejo, was coaching in Old Havana, and invited Namibia to his open-air gym. Ramos, thirty-four, was a heavyweight who'd had to retire because he tried to escape from the island by sea so that he could fight on the international circuit. He got caught, and the Cuban Boxing Federation disqualified him from competition.

In front of Damián's house on Calle Cárdenas was a collapsed tenement. On one of its walls was an old mural of a Cuban flag with Che Guevara's face and his phrase *Hasta La Victoria Siempre*! (Ever Onward to Victory!) Inside was a courtyard which Damián had turned into a ring. It was here that I saw Namibia spar against a twenty-six-year-old man. Afterward, tired from the fight, she told me, "You know, you win when you lose a round, because it teaches you how to be better. My errors have all made me stronger."

Damián only coached Namibia twice a week. But Maykel Masó, another retired boxer Namibia knew from Rafael Trejo, was coaching on a nearby rooftop on Calle Sol. He trains Havana's under-eighteen fighters, but during the pandemic, his outdoor gym gave Namibia a chance to box. Maykel says that Namibia was always explosive, and that her speed was what initially caught his attention. She's not so quick now, but her arms are still shockingly strong.

After warming up and doing some group exercises, Maykel has his students pair up to spar. I watch them on a late afternoon, close to sunset. Namibia pairs up with Bárbaro, a fifteen-year-old southpaw who's a big hope in lightweight boxing. Thirty years younger than Namibia, he's a highly developed boxer, with arms like tentacles that won't let her into the fight. She can't get close, can't fool him, and she loses her composure and lets her guard down. He hits her with punishing jabs. Namibia gets angry, not at him—his hits are clean—but at her powerlessness against time.

Maykel intervenes, telling them to relax, it's a warmup. Namibia snaps at Bárbaro, "If you touch my face, I'm really going to get pissed." Maykel then gives the fighters two minutes to rest. "Life is like boxing," Namibia says, taking her gloves off. "You don't lose if you get knocked down; you lose if you don't get back up." Her hands are wrapped to the fingertips in yellowed bandages that drip sweat. She walks to the corner of the roof with her gloves under her right arm. The sun hits her face, and, squinting, she leans forward and looks down at people on the doorstep below. A cop car circles. A teenage couple kisses desperately.

"I don't feel sorry so much as empty," Namibia says. "I'll always wonder what could have happened to me, but all I can do is accept who I am now." Then she puts her gloves back on.

Editor's Note: In December 2022, the Cuban Boxing Federation finally lifted the ban on female boxing in the country and announced the formation of a national women's team. The goal was for the team to compete in the 2024 Olympics in Paris, but because of the lack of training time, none of the female Cuban boxers qualified for the games.

EPILOGUE: JOURNEY TO ANOTHER WORLD

I wasn't prepared for my last house arrest. In my head, I had already left Cuba, and so I wasn't ready when a carload of cops and plainclothes security agents descended on my home to prevent me from covering a protest scheduled for November 15th, 2021.

The house arrest brought me back to reality. It also sent me into a crisis of anxiety. My whole body hurt. My ribcage felt as if there was a knife stuck in it. It was as if my head wasn't working, or had been disconnected from the rest of me. An uncontrollable rage took over. Later, my therapist explained to me that anger is the other side of sorrow, and I was, indeed, very sad. My grief was consuming me.

Since June 2016, I had been subjected to migratory regulation, prohibiting me from leaving Cuba. "Migratory regulation" is a Castroist term. It's one of the government's ways of retaliating against anyone that crosses them: denying that person the ability to leave the island, which, aside from the end of the dictatorship, is what most Cubans want. We aren't especially avid travelers; we just want progress, which is available only if we emigrate, and even those uninterested in living elsewhere hope for a chance to breathe freely, to supply ourselves with oxygen abroad before we dive anew into the dark well of totalitarianism.

Migratory regulation wasn't the only repressive technique the government used to try to force me to give up my journalism, but it was the worst: worse than house arrests, arbitrary interrogations and the occasional kidnapping; worse than harassing my friends and family, threatening to jail me, slandering me on the news, reading my correspondence. In a country that treats independent journalists as if we were terrorists, not being allowed to leave is itself a form of political imprisonment.

For two decades, migratory regulation was the government's preferred punishment for those who opposed the regime. However, by forbidding dissidents to leave, the government unwittingly created an island full of angry people, armed with the internet. This suppressed anger exploded in July 2021, leading to the biggest anti-government protests in Castroism's seventy-three-year history.

Seeing its citizens in the streets showed the state that it needed a new strategy. Rather than trapping dissenters on the island, the regime decided to get rid of them. Freedom in exchange for exile. As a result, nearly all the members of the civil society that arose online in the mid-2010s have left Cuba, and those who remain are either in prison or otherwise bound and restrained by the government.

* * *

Before I became "regulated," I had never left Cuba because, until 2013, it was very difficult to do so. You had to request permission from the state, which could easily be denied, and even if you got it, you still had to pay $100 for a passport, which was far more than I could afford at the time. (I was writing for a magazine called *OnCuba*, getting paid $3 per article.)

My departure from Cuba began with a call from a blocked number. I answered and heard a man yelling. I couldn't understand a word he said. He didn't introduce himself. As I was about to hang up, he said, "passport."

In that moment, I remembered that all the calls I'd received from state security—threats, orders to show up at a certain police station at a certain time to be interrogated—came from blocked numbers. I asked the man who he was, but he ignored me and continued yelling. I finally made out, "Don't you get it? You can have a passport! Go apply!"

He went quiet, and I had no idea how to reply. Eventually, he asked, "Aren't you going to thank me?"

"I don't have to thank anybody for giving me back a right that was taken away," I said, and then I hung up.

I sat in my living room, neither happy nor surprised. Maybe I would have felt better if the man hadn't asked me if I was going to thank him. But his request, or demand, made me feel pathetic. I saw myself as a slave, a loser, a worm, to use the word the regime prefers for its opponents. I was still subject to the government's universal, oppressive control.

* * *

Life in Cuba is absurd, and all that those who live here can do is try and adapt to it, accustomed as we are to the horrors Castroism relies on to perpetuate itself. For proof, consider the start of this epilogue: I wasn't prepared for my last house arrest. A person who writes that assumes that arbitrary house arrest is normal. A person who writes that comes from a position of legal helplessness. A person who writes that is attempting to defend himself by speaking out, since that's the only option he's got. A person who writes that lives in a state of constant readiness of being repressed, since he's chosen to be a political entity in a country where that means you'd better be ready for the worst.

* * *

A few days later, I decided to go to the Ministry of the Interior's passport department to see if I really was no longer regulated. At the time, there was a pandemic curfew prohibiting citizens from leaving their homes between 9:00 p.m. and 5:00 a.m. I went out before five, carrying my coffee in a paper cup, and saw lines forming outside every store and market, full of people sneaking out during curfew, hiding in bushes, culverts, alleys and shadows so that they wouldn't get arrested trying to beat the morning rush to buy the little food available that day.

I got to the Ministry of the Interior at ten past five. I was the sixth in line to apply for a passport. Slowly the waiting area grew crowded with others trying to obtain or renew their passports. It wasn't until eight o'clock that my turn came. A sleepy woman asked for my documents and entered my information into her computer. I doubted that I would progress any further. I'd gotten this far before, and had always been told I was regulated. But this time, the woman yawned and, not raising her eyes, returned my papers and said, "Next room for fingerprints." I was in. It had started.

As I completed the application process, my heart rose. The mysterious caller had been right. In fifteen days, I would return for my passport.

* * *

I showed up on the appointed day, again setting off before five in the morning with my coffee. When I heard my name and went up to the counter, a man handed me a small blue booklet with República de Cuba embossed on its cover. I was shocked. Astonishing that a little leaflet could mean so much.

Shortly after, I was invited to Amsterdam to give a talk and be on a panel on journalism and freedom of speech. I'd received many such invitations before, but I'd always had to decline or participate virtually. My depression initially began with all the "no" RSVPs. I saw how many opportunities for career growth I was missing, how many events I didn't have the freedom to attend, how much I was drowning within the Cuban state.

At the Dutch embassy, I had to wait with a handful of other visa applicants. While the woman before me took her turn, an embassy staffer told me to go wash my hands, which was part of their pandemic protocols. In the bathroom, I had, for the first time in my life, the sense that I was no longer in Cuba. It was the biggest, most beautiful bathroom I had ever seen, with a toilet in one corner and a sink in the other. I could see my reflection as clearly in the shining floor tile as I could in the mirror on the wall. It smelled like anything but a bathroom.

After washing my hands, I was surprised not to see a way to dry them. By the sink was an apparatus that, it occurred to me, could be one of those air-blowing hand dryers I'd seen in movies. But I couldn't get it to turn on. I hit its side as if it were one of the black-and-white TVs of my childhood, which you'd smack if the signal went out. I struggled with the dryer until the staffer knocked on the door and said, "Sir, it's your turn."

Panicked, I ran to the toilet, pulled some paper from the roll, and dried my hands—or tried to. Of course, what happened was that I emerged with the hands of a mummy, covered in damp paper.

A very kind woman helped me through the application process. Surely she saw how anxious I was; before we began, she asked, "Is this your first time?" She looked at my documents, asked her questions, and then got out a fingerprint scanner. However, when I touched the machine, it shut down. How could it not? My hands were covered in wet toilet paper.

"I don't know what's wrong," the woman said. Hiding my

hands behind my back, I said that I didn't know either. She restarted the scanner, and I surreptitiously wiped my hands on my pants, getting them, if not fully paper-free, into a state the machine could manage when it turned back on.

* * *

We Cubans get used to living under repression, to seeing our friends and family mistreated, which, of course, leaves scars, but for me, the hardest part of my regulated years was how alone I became. All my friends left Cuba. My childhood neighbors left. My university classmates left. My colleagues left. I ended up knowing very few people in the country—and those who I did know were too afraid of government reprisals to see me.

My solitude reached a level where I went months without speaking to anyone but my immediate family. I left my house only to walk or run, which reminded me that I lived in a nation of ghosts. I thought constantly of my friends who'd left. Nighttime was the worst. When I eventually fell asleep, I dreamed of images and landscapes that made me feel isolated, trapped, shut away on the island with my family. I'd wake up in the dark, sweating and agitated, too afraid of returning to those dreams to fall asleep again.

On my last birthday in Cuba, I didn't have a single person to invite. I used to treat birthdays as an excuse to have everyone I knew over. This time, I looked through photos of earlier parties, a concession to nostalgia that demonstrated how empty my life had become: every year, more people were gone, until finally the only person left was me.

My last house arrest, which lasted seventy-two hours, was the hardest. The loneliness sent me into panic attacks. Once I was released, I went out for a walk with no destination and found myself at the José Martí Stadium, a decrepit, defunct sports complex on the Malecón. I used to play soccer there with my university friends every weekend. It's in such bad shape that there's a guard keeping people out, but I asked him for permission to enter, which he granted. Carefully, I ascended the stands and sat for a while, contemplating the abandoned fields and splintering bleachers. Later, as I left, the guard said, "Brother, it's a graveyard in there."

* * *

Then my events in Amsterdam were postponed. I was so close to an exit, and now I was blocked. I kept thinking that some superhuman force didn't want me to leave, that I was going to be marooned in Cuba until I died.

I had my visa, but the Omicron variant of the coronavirus was spreading worldwide. Concerned that it would cause countries to close their borders, I decided to go to Spain to wait for my Dutch events to be rescheduled. I just couldn't take it any more on the island.

I had to grit my teeth through each moment until I got to the airport, where I met a welcome party of state security agents in disguise. I recognized them because they tailed me from the moment I got out of the taxi, and because one of them had been part of my last house arrest. As they followed me, they talked incessantly on their phones. I would've been on edge regardless due to my inexperience in airports, but the agents' presence convinced me that I wasn't going to be allowed to leave.

At security, I created a giant backup because I didn't know I had to put each of my electronic devices and metal objects in its own bin. When they went through the scanning tunnel, I chased after them, not wanting them to spill onto the floor. Everyone laughed at me but the gate agent, who grabbed me by the arm and showed me the body scanner I'd failed to walk through.

Once I was at my gate, though, I relaxed somewhat. Boarding began; I walked down the cold jet bridge, and lo and behold, I was on the plane. I was leaving Cuba.

* * *

Leaving Cuba isn't like leaving any other country. Leaving Cuba means landing in the world. Leaving Cuba shows you that the island has been held hostage in the twentieth century by a political system that won't let it move forward. Citizens of most other countries aren't violently shaken by travel, since their lives, to varying degrees, obey the logic of contemporary societies. Cuban-ness, on the other hand, is a serious condition.

When I got out of the plane in Madrid, I immediately knew that I was opening the door to a new world.

Madrid was just a layover—my final destination was Barcelona, where I live today. I felt like a phantom from the moment I arrived. Strange stimuli muddied my thoughts. I was nauseous. My temples pounded constantly. My surroundings seemed faraway and surreal, as if I were in a movie.

After a few weeks, it occurred to me that my head hurt because I wasn't letting my eyes rest. I was looking at every single thing. I still do. On the streets, I look at every bar, every coffee shop, every restaurant, every sign, every store, every person, every person's mouth speaking its many different languages. It's a captivating amount of information, too much for my poor eyes. My vision comes from Cuba, where reality is colorless and monolithic.

One day, I went into a bookstore in the Raval neighborhood that was packed with high shelves heavy with books. I couldn't read the titles: the letters swam. Suddenly I imagined a shelf collapsing and crushing me. I bolted from the store, heart racing, and sat on a bench with some pigeons. My panic wasn't an isolated event; it was what my new world was doing to me.

I had never been a foreigner before. Now I'm so foreign, so alien to the world I move through, that I feel as if I'll never learn to belong. If I'm not careful, I stare at passersby like you would an exotic animal. I'm not quite sure why, but my guess is that it has to do with their clothes. People dress very differently in Spain than in Cuba, which makes sense: Cubans can hardly buy food, let alone nice clothing.

I'm struck by the dogs, too. I keep seeing breeds I recognize from movies. I brought this up to a college friend who lives here, and he said, "You're not noticing them because of their breeds. What you're noticing is that the dogs at home are aggressive. Here, they've got manners."

My agitation has ruined my appetite. In Cuba, we eat badly or not at all. Here, food is everywhere. The variety and quantity of options are so extreme that my mind can't handle it. If I'm brave enough to enter a market, I last only a moment before hurrying out, eyes on the floor, alarmed by the mountains of choices. I come from a place where you eat whatever there is. I don't know how to choose between so many yogurts, so many juices, so much of everything.

It's the same with other kinds of shopping. I arrived here in winter with nothing to wear, since "cold" in the Caribbean means seventy-five degrees. Some friends loaned me clothes while I worked up the nerve to enter a store and buy what I needed. I'm still afraid of shopping. When I walk by a store, I glance out of the corner of my eye at the overwhelming excess of outfits and mannequins.

Speaking of walking, I keep nearly being run over. At first, I didn't know that the sidewalks had special bike lanes, so I'd walk in them, and would nearly get hit by bicycles or electric scooters. While it took me less time to figure out that every single street, even the small ones, has a crossing light, I still have a hard time traversing big avenues. It goes against my instincts to keep walking ahead, and so, in the middle of crosswalks, I instinctively dodge one person and knock into another. Before long I'm hopelessly tangled, surrounded by people who I can tell want to know what's wrong with me, why I keep bumping into them.

* * *

One night, a friend invited me over for drinks. I decided this was a great opportunity to ride the metro by myself, which I'd never done before. I descended the stairs into the station, consulted the map, and tried to go through the turnstile, but my card wouldn't swipe. I glanced around at the other people until I figured out that I wasn't doing it right: I was waving my card over the slot, not holding it underneath like the other commuters. When I finally did it correctly, the gate sucked my card in so quickly that I jumped as if a dog had bitten me. By the time I regained my composure, the turnstile had opened and closed, and I couldn't insert my card again; you have to wait fifteen minutes, I later learned.

I went to the help kiosk, if that's what its called, and explained my situation. Luckily, the woman who was working there sympathized with my plight and used her card to let me in. I went down the next set of stairs just as a train was arriving, but I wasn't sure it was mine. I asked a man, who said I had to go to the other track. When I got there, I looked at the map, but didn't see my stop. I was beset by such anxiety that I had to get above ground. I ended up taking a taxi to my friend's house.

* * *

We drank beer until midnight, which was later than I'd intended to stay. I wanted to walk home, so I pulled up Google Maps—also new to me—and headed out. When I thought I was about halfway there, I consulted the route on my phone and found that not only had I gone in the wrong direction, but my avatar also wasn't moving the same way I was. For fifteen minutes, I paced the same block, my avatar going right every time I went left. I couldn't figure out how to fix it. Furious and frightened, I shouted a curse so Cuban that a couple walking by stopped and asked, "Are you from Cuba?"

"I am," I answered, embarrassed, "and I'm lost."

They were Cuban, too. They took my phone, showed me how to use the app, and accompanied me for a little while, telling me that it had been ten years since they'd been on the island, but that they were thinking of visiting soon.

After we said goodbye, I noticed how cold I was. My phone said it was thirty-seven degrees. Overhead, a billboard caught my eye. *Vida Nova*, it said. It was an ad for wine.

A few days later, I bought myself some winter clothes. I took this as a sign that I was improving emotionally.

* * *

My next shopping trip happened after a Catalan friend invited me to join his nighttime soccer game. I'd never really played soccer after sunset before, because in Cuba, there are no fields or stadiums with lights. My friends and I did sometimes play in darkness to satisfy our soccer addiction, but that was very different from this game, in which there was so much illumination that if the ball went high into the air, I had to shield my eyes with my hand, as if I were staring into the sun at the beach, to see it. A few times, the goalie kicked me the ball and I had to pretend I couldn't get to it quickly enough because I was afraid that, blinded by the lights, I'd receive it poorly, and in soccer, there's no truer measure of your skill than whether you can trap a ball coming from above.

Before the game, my friend told me I needed something called "multitacos" so that I wouldn't slip on the Astroturf, which was completely new to me. I assumed that he was talking about a kind of shoe with cleats you can switch out for different surfaces, like track spikes. But no: I went to a sporting goods store and asked for "multitacos," which turned out to be special shoes exclusively for playing soccer on artificial turf.

Arriving at the field, I warmed up for a long time, nervous about my balance in my new turf shoes. It felt like I was learning to skate. While I jogged and stretched, I asked one of my new teammates if it was normal for advertisers to encourage compulsive consumption—at the sporting goods store, I'd seen a sign that said, "Welcome Shopping Addicts." Reading that hit me hard. It was like a message from my new world. Of course, I knew that capitalism was based on consumption, but I didn't understand how overt it was. Until that moment, I'd been innocent enough to assume that such intentions were hidden, at least.

Now I can't stop noticing how capitalism—I'm aware that I'm not breaking new ground here—transforms humans into compulsive consumers. I saw it in action when shopping for winter clothes in an enormous, multilevel department store designed to be difficult to leave. I spent more time trying to go up or down a floor than I did trying on clothes. When I decided what to purchase, it was mainly out of overwhelm—and, of course, my route from checkout to exit was full of nicer clothes than the ones I'd selected, tempting me to shop even more.

I have become obsessed with consumption. When I pass a bakery, I wonder how long all the breads and pastries—more than anyone could possibly sell or eat—remain on sale. One time I asked a baker about this, and he told me that you can only sell an item for up to twenty-four hours after it emerges from the oven. After that, everything is thrown away—though Barcelona has recently launched an effort to send these goods to soup kitchens.

A woman lives on the sidewalk outside one of the bakeries near my apartment. I'm fairly certain she's Arab. She always has a sign that says, in green marker, "God doesn't love me because he doesn't help me. Please help me get something to eat." Recently I was coming home late at night and saw her asleep on a heap of rags, with more rags on top of her to keep her warm. A foot or two away, a man in an apron and white hat was throwing out two full trays of croissants.

I'm drawn to people like that woman. It's not misery porn or gloating or hypocrisy; I just want to know how someone gets to this point, sleeping on the street, covered in rags, begging for help. Most of them seem to be immigrants, and I want to know how they got here from Africa, or the Arab world, or—this one is less frequent here—Latin America. I never dare to ask them, as it seems cruel.

One time, however, I did speak to someone who was living "rough"—a term I prefer, for unknown reasons, to homeless or beggar. I was meeting a musician friend at a bar, and when I arrived, he was talking to a Cameroonian woman who'd asked him for money. He'd said that instead of money, he'd buy her whatever she wanted. She requested a soda, and while he went to the bar, I spoke with the woman, asking how she was, where she was from and how long she'd been in Spain.

She had a question for me, too. "Where are you from?" she asked. "You're just as Black as me." To her, our Blackness both linked us and made my concern for her irrelevant. She thought I should worry about myself. I experience this often when talking to other immigrants: any questions I ask get taken as a cry for help, not curiosity, and before long they're advising me to get a job as a driver, a security guard or an Amazon deliveryman.

* * *

That ended up being one of worst nights of my life. My friend and I had some beers, said goodbye, and left the bar. Only when I was out in the cold did I realize that I had to pee. Since leaving Cuba, this has become an issue. Part of the problem is that Europeans generally drink wine in the winter, but I don't especially like wine, so I stick to beer, and so my bladder's always full. But even when I haven't been drinking, which is most of the time, I have to pee nonstop. It's miserable.

I went into the metro station and looked for a bathroom, but couldn't find one. I told myself that I could manage the eight stops until I got home. It was late, and there were only four other riders in my car. A few minutes later, I felt a sharp pain in my pelvis. I had to stand and pace to avoid wetting my pants. A drop of urine slid down my leg. I glanced around to see if anyone was looking: one person was, which made me panic. I got off the train one stop early. I could already feel my pants and socks starting to get wet, but once on the platform, my body relaxed completely and I started peeing.

Outside the station, the air was dry and hideously cold. When I pulled out my phone, it was dead, and I had no idea where I was. I raised my eyes and didn't see a single star. I wanted to cry. I was shivering, lost, and covered in piss. My chest tightened, the start of a panic attack. I was too ashamed to approach anyone who'd left the station with me. Soon I was alone in the street. I waited a long time for another person to appear, a woman who, understandably, didn't want to talk to a strange man who approached her in the night.

I walked ten blocks in a random direction, longing for Google Maps, before managing to hail a taxi. When I got home, I laid down on the floor, not even bothering to take off my clothes. I felt like the saddest man in the world.

* * *

When I finally made it to Amsterdam, I was nervous about my talk and panel, because I wasn't sure what sort of crowd to anticipate and because I'd never done events like these in person before. I'm also not great at public speaking; I like to chat and listen, but not with everyone's eyes on me.

During my second event, a man slipped into the back of the auditorium. He looked like a Cuban state security agent: unfashionable clothes that were neither tight nor loose, thick glasses, notebook in hand, malice on his face. In the middle of my presentation, he began demanding to speak. He was told he had to wait until the Q&A segment. When his turn came, rather than asking anything, he insulted me. He said I was a liar; that Cubans had civil rights, including the right to practice journalism; that no Cubans were in jail for protesting; that no one gets kicked out of the country; that it's an island paradise. Because the man didn't ask me a questions, I didn't reply, which annoyed him.

After the event, I went to the bathroom—you'll be shocked to learn that I had to pee—and he was waiting for me when I came out. He let loose another barrage of insults. I attempted to listen to him, to have some sort of dialogue, but I eventually accepted that it wasn't possible and headed to the bar. He followed me, shouting abuse, until the panel's organizers came to my rescue. Later, a diplomat friend showed me a photo of the man at the Cuban embassy in the Netherlands. He'd been sent to make a scene.

* * *

The evening I arrived in Amsterdam, I asked a friend to take me to the city's Red Light District. Walking around there scrambled my brain. I couldn't believe I was seeing women flaunting their bodies in windows, sucking their fingers, posing for spectators, inviting strangers to pay to penetrate their bodies or watch them masturbate in dim, red-bulbed rooms. My Dutch friend told me that although the work the women does is legal, and although they pay taxes, it remains looked down upon. Apparently the state permits it in an effort to prevent human trafficking and regulate prostitution, but neither of those goals has been achieved, and now they're in a mess they don't know how to get out of. I was up all night after that, considering the thought that liberty could have its limits.

I returned to Barcelona with renewed energy. My experience in the Red Light District had given me a philosophical problem to consider, instead of my basic concerns with the metro, Google Maps, the heaps of food and goods for sale and the swarms of people on the street.

* * *

My next trip took me back to Madrid. A good friend of mine who lived there had promised, in the years I was regulated and had no hope of leaving Cuba, that when I did leave, he'd take me to a soccer game at Santiago Bernabéu Stadium. Now he'd gotten us tickets.

While I was in the city, I took care of some professional business and saw some people that I loved, including my therapist. She had saved me in my time of greatest despondence, and I wanted to thank her in person. We'd never met face to face, as all our sessions were virtual. Before starting therapy with her, my psychologist on the island had abandoned me after the regime had its news station call me "a paid agent of the CIA and foreign governments." I sought treatment from other Cuban therapists, but they all said no for fear of reprisals. I then reached out to the Committee to Protect Journalists, and they put me in contact with my therapist.

We met for a coffee and hugged immediately, then talked for nearly an hour. Sunlight kept shining into my face, reminding me of our sessions in Havana, which all took place on my roof: it was the only place I got good enough internet for her image not to freeze.

During the same trip, I met two Cuban colleagues at the Plaza Puerto del Sol. As I was walking there, a girl in her early twenties stopped me. We were in the center of Madrid, amid a swarming hive of people. She wanted my information for some sort of marketing scheme. I told her I didn't have an address to give her; I was brand new to Spain.

"Where are you from?" she asked.

"Cuba."

"Me too! My mom and I came here when I was two, though, and I've never been back."

She thanked me for paying attention to her, knocked her elbow into mine as a goodbye and wished me luck. As I started to walk away, I turned to see her already engaged with another person.

In the plaza, the crowds were so dense I was reminded of school outings to the Malecón, when we'd have to dress up and sing songs to commemorate some miniscule milestone or satisfy a whim of Castro's—though in those cases, unlike in the Plaza Puerto del Sol, I didn't bump into people dressed like Buzz Lightyear or Mickey Mouse.

* * *

The day I left Madrid, I walked to the train station, wanting to see more of the city before departing. On the Paseo de la Castellana, I heard a commotion that turned out to be a protest. Madrid's left was demonstrating against corruption in the *Partido Popular,* or People's Party, a Christian conservative political party in Spain. I sat on my suitcase and watched the march as if it were theater. It was theater to me, a scene I'd never witnessed: police protecting rather than abusing the protestors; protestors waving signs that stated clearly what they wanted; a band; old people; children. I couldn't help thinking of the more than 1400 people who remained in jail in Cuba for doing the same thing in 2021.

After the march was over, I got up to go to the train station, pausing at a souvenir stand. While I was browsing, my mother texted me to say that my grandmother had just been hospitalized in Havana. She died a few days later. She was eighty-three and had never left Cuba.

www.ingramcontent.com/pod-product-compliance
Lightning Source LLC
Jackson TN
JSHW021736110725
87411JS00001B/1
9781632462091